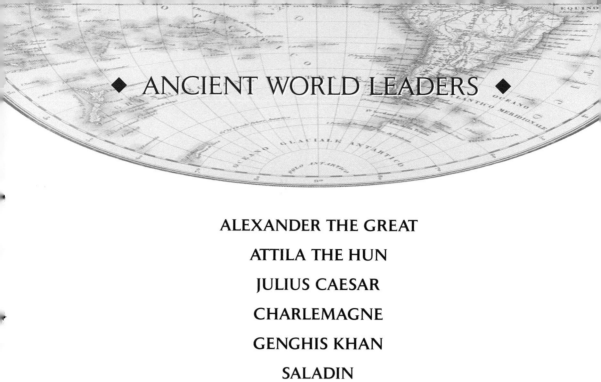

◆ ANCIENT WORLD LEADERS ◆

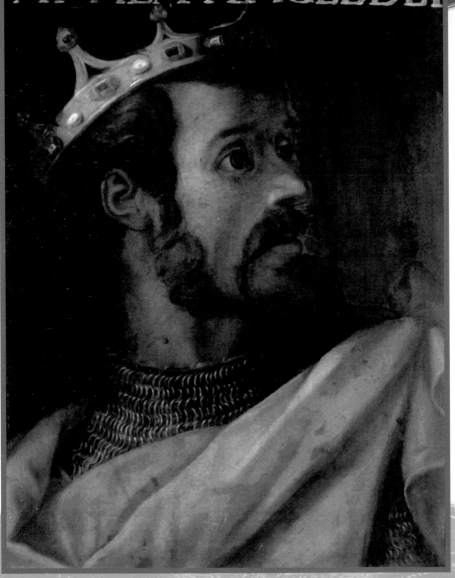

ATTILA FLAGEL:DEI

ATTILA THE HUN

◆◆◆

Bonnie Carman Harvey

CHELSEA HOUSE
PUBLISHERS
A Haights Cross Communications ◆ Company

Philadelphia

Frontispiece: Attila the Hun, known as the "Scourge of God" to his victims in the Western world, would go on to become one of the most feared Mongol conquerors from the east.

CHELSEA HOUSE PUBLISHERS

VP, NEW PRODUCT DEVELOPMENT Sally Cheney
DIRECTOR OF PRODUCTION Kim Shinners
CREATIVE MANAGER Takeshi Takahashi
MANUFACTURING MANAGER Diann Grasse

Staff for ATTILA THE HUN

ASSOCIATE EDITOR Benjamin Xavier Kim
PRODUCTION EDITOR Jaimie Winkler
PICTURE RESEARCHER Pat Holl
SERIES DESIGNER Takeshi Takahashi
COVER DESIGNER Keith Trego
LAYOUT 21st Century Publishing and Communications, Inc.

A Haights Cross Communications ✈ Company

http://www.chelseahouse.com

First Printing

1 3 5 7 9 8 6 4 2

Library of Congress Cataloging-in-Publication Data

Harvey, Bonnie C.
  Attila, the Hun / Bonnie Harvey.
      p. cm. -- (Ancient world leaders)
Includes index.
ISBN 0-7910-7221-5 HC   0-7910-7495-1 PB
Summary: Describes the life of Attila, leader of the Huns, and his attempt to conquer the Roman Empire. 1. Attila, d. 453--Juvenile literature. 2. Huns--Biography--Juvenile literature. 3. Huns--History--Juvenile literature. [1. Attila, d. 453 2. Kings, queens, rulers, etc. 3. Huns--History.] I. Title. II. Series.

  D141.H35 2003
  936--dc21

                                                              2002155106

TABLE OF CONTENTS

ON LEADERSHIP

Arthur M. Schlesinger, jr.

Leadership, it may be said, is really what makes the world go round. Love no doubt smoothes the passage; but love is a private transaction between consenting adults. Leadership is a public transaction with history. The idea of leadership affirms the capacity of individuals to move, inspire, and mobilize masses of people so that they act together in pursuit of an end. Sometimes leadership serves good purposes, sometimes bad; but whether the end is benign or evil, great leaders are those men and women who leave their personal stamp on history.

Now, the very concept of leadership implies the proposition that individuals can make a difference. This proposition has never been universally accepted. From classical times to the present day, eminent thinkers have regarded individuals as no more than the agents and pawns of larger forces, whether the gods and goddesses of the ancient world or, in the modern era, race, class, nation, the dialectic, the will of the people, the spirit of the times, history itself. Against such forces, the individual dwindles into insignificance.

So contends the thesis of historical determinism. Tolstoy's great novel *War and Peace* offers a famous statement of the case. Why, Tolstoy asked, did millions of men in the Napoleonic Wars, denying their human feelings and their common sense, move back and forth across Europe slaughtering their fellows? "The war," Tolstoy answered, "was bound to happen simply because it was bound to happen." All prior history determined it. As for leaders, they, Tolstoy said, "are but the labels that serve to give a name to an end and, like labels, they have the least possible connection with the event." The greater the leader, "the more conspicuous the inevitability and the predestination of every act he commits." The leader, said Tolstoy, is "the slave of history."

Determinism takes many forms. Marxism is the determinism of class, Nazism is the determinism of race. But the idea of men and women as the slaves of history runs athwart the deepest human instincts. Rigid determinism abolishes the idea of human freedom—the assumption of free choice that underlies every move we make, every word we speak, every thought we think. It abolishes the idea of human responsibility, since it is manifestly unfair to reward or punish people for actions that are by definition beyond their control. No one can live consistently by any deterministic creed. The Marxist states prove this themselves by their extreme susceptibility to the cult of leadership.

More than that, history refutes the idea that individuals make no difference. In December 1931, a British politician crossing Fifth Avenue in New York City between 76th and 77th Streets around 10:30 P.M. looked in the wrong direction and was knocked down by an automobile— a moment, he later recalled, of a man aghast, a world aglare: "I do not understand why I was not broken like an eggshell or squashed like a gooseberry." Fourteen months later an American politician, sitting in an open car in Miami, Florida, was fired on by an assassin; the man beside him was hit. Those who believe that individuals make no difference to history might well ponder whether the next two decades would have been the same had Mario Constasino's car killed Winston Churchill in 1931 and Giuseppe Zangara's bullet killed Franklin Roosevelt in 1933. Suppose, in addition, that Lenin had died of typhus in Siberia in 1895 and that Hitler had been killed on the western front in 1916. What would the 20th century have looked like now?

For better or for worse, individuals do make a difference. "The notion that a people can run itself and its affairs anonymously," wrote the philosopher William James, "is now well known to be the silliest of absurdities. Mankind does nothing save through initiatives on the part of inventors, great or small, and imitation by the rest of us—these are the sole factors in human progress. Individuals of genius show the way, and set the patterns, which common people then adopt and follow."

Leadership, James suggests, means leadership in thought as well as in action. In the long run, leaders in thought may well make the greater difference to the world. "The ideas of economists and political philoso-phers, both when they are right and when they are wrong," wrote John Maynard Keynes, "are more powerful than is commonly understood. Indeed the world is ruled by little else. Practical men, who believe them-selves to be quite exempt from any intellectual influences, are usually the slaves of some defunct economist. . . . The power of vested interests is vastly exaggerated compared with the gradual encroachment of ideas."

But, as Woodrow Wilson once said, "Those only are leaders of men, in the general eye, who lead in action. . . . It is at their hands that new thought gets its translation into the crude language of deeds." Leaders in thought often invent in solitude and obscurity, leaving to later generations the tasks of imitation. Leaders in action—the leaders portrayed in this series—have to be effective in their own time.

And they cannot be effective by themselves. They must act in response to the rhythms of their age. Their genius must be adapted, in a phrase from William James, "to the receptivities of the moment." Leaders are useless without followers. "There goes the mob," said the French politician, hearing a clamor in the streets. "I am their leader. I must follow them." Great leaders turn the inchoate emotions of the mob to purposes of their own. They seize on the opportunities of their time, the hopes, fears, frustrations, crises, potentialities. They succeed when events have prepared the way for them, when the community is awaiting to be aroused, when they can provide the clarifying and organizing ideas. Leadership completes the circuit between the individual and the mass and thereby alters history.

It may alter history for better or for worse. Leaders have been responsible for the most extravagant follies and most monstrous crimes that have beset suffering humanity. They have also been vital in such gains as humanity has made in individual freedom, religious and racial tolerance, social justice, and respect for human rights.

There is no sure way to tell in advance who is going to lead for good and who for evil. But a glance at the gallery of men and women in ANCIENT WORLD LEADERS suggests some useful tests.

One test is this: Do leaders lead by force or by persuasion? By command or by consent? Through most of history leadership was exercised by the divine right of authority. The duty of followers was to defer and to obey. "Theirs not to reason why/Theirs but to do and die." On occasion, as with the so-called enlightened despots of the 18th century in Europe, absolutist leadership was animated by humane purposes. More often, absolutism nourished the passion for domination, land, gold, and conquest and resulted in tyranny.

The great revolution of modern times has been the revolution of equality. "Perhaps no form of government," wrote the British historian James Bryce in his study of the United States, *The American Commonwealth*, "needs great leaders so much as democracy." The idea that all people should be equal in their legal condition has undermined the old structure of authority, hierarchy, and deference. The revolution of equality has had two contrary effects on the nature of leadership. For equality, as Alexis de Tocqueville pointed out in his great study *Democracy in America*, might mean equality in servitude as well as equality in freedom.

"I know of only two methods of establishing equality in the political world," Tocqueville wrote. "Rights must be given to every citizen, or none at all to anyone . . . save one, who is the master of all." There was no middle ground "between the sovereignty of all and the absolute power of one man." In his astonishing prediction of 20th-century totalitarian dictatorship, Tocqueville explained how the revolution of equality could lead to the *Führerprinzip* and more terrible absolutism than the world had ever known.

But when rights are given to every citizen and the sovereignty of all is established, the problem of leadership takes a new form, becomes more exacting than ever before. It is easy to issue commands and enforce them by the rope and the stake, the concentration camp and the *gulag*. It is much harder to use argument and achievement to overcome opposition and win consent. The Founding Fathers of the United States understood the difficulty. They believed that history had given them the opportunity to decide, as Alexander Hamilton wrote in the first Federalist Paper, whether men are indeed capable of basing government on "reflection and choice, or whether they are forever destined to depend . . . on accident and force."

Government by reflection and choice called for a new style of leadership and a new quality of followership. It required leaders to be responsive to popular concerns, and it required followers to be active and informed participants in the process. Democracy does not eliminate emotion from politics; sometimes it fosters demagoguery; but it is confident that, as the greatest of democratic leaders put it, you cannot fool all of the people all of the time. It measures leadership by results and retires those who overreach or falter or fail.

It is true that in the long run despots are measured by results too. But they can postpone the day of judgment, sometimes indefinitely, and in the meantime they can do infinite harm. It is also true that democracy is no guarantee of virtue and intelligence in government, for the voice of the people is not necessarily the voice of God. But democracy, by assuring the right of opposition, offers built-in resistance to the evils inherent in absolutism. As the theologian Reinhold Niebuhr summed it up, "Man's capacity for justice makes democracy possible, but man's inclination to justice makes democracy necessary."

A second test for leadership is the end for which power is sought. When leaders have as their goal the supremacy of a master race or the promotion of totalitarian revolution or the acquisition and exploitation of colonies or the protection of greed and privilege or the preservation of personal power, it is likely that their leadership will do little to advance the cause of humanity. When their goal is the abolition of slavery, the liberation of women, the enlargement of opportunity for the poor and powerless, the extension of equal rights to racial minorities, the defense of the freedoms of expression and opposition, it is likely that their leadership will increase the sum of human liberty and welfare.

Leaders have done great harm to the world. They have also conferred great benefits. You will find both sorts in this series. Even "good" leaders must be regarded with a certain wariness. Leaders are not demigods; they put on their trousers one leg after another just like ordinary mortals. No leader is infallible, and every leader needs to be reminded of this at regular intervals. Irreverence irritates leaders but is their salvation. Unquestioning submission corrupts leaders and demeans followers. Making a cult of a leader is always a mistake. Fortunately hero worship generates its own antidote. "Every hero," said Emerson, "becomes a bore at last."

The single benefit the great leaders confer is to embolden the rest of us to live according to our own best selves, to be active, insistent, and resolute in affirming our own sense of things. For great leaders attest to the reality of human freedom against the supposed inevitabilities of history. And they attest to the wisdom and power that may lie within the most unlikely of us, which is why Abraham Lincoln remains the supreme example of great leadership. A great leader, said Emerson, exhibits new possibilities to all humanity. "We feed on genius . . . . Great men exist that there may be greater men."

Great leaders, in short, justify themselves by emancipating and empowering their followers. So humanity struggles to master its destiny, remembering with Alexis de Tocqueville: "It is true that around every man a fatal circle is traced beyond which he cannot pass; but within the wide verge of that circle he is powerful and free; as it is with man, so with communities." ■

The TRACKS of various MIGRATING & RAIDING PEOPLES

between 1AD and 700AD

Circles represent phases of settlement. The reader must bear in mind that there was also an annual north-&-south oscillation, (between summer & winter pastures) of all the nomadic peoples...

Inset Map showing GOTHIC Migrations separately.

THE SCOURGE
OF GOD

Thousands of warriors on horseback charged across the sandy plains with the dust kicked up by the horses' hooves blotting out the sun. The Ostrogoths reported that they had been attacked by strange-looking men who "were hideous to behold; skulls deformed by binding when young and slits for eyes. [They had] swollen cheeks disfigured by scars and covered in wispy hair."

Known as "Huns," the horses and their riders were so in tune with each other they seemed to move as a unit. The short, shaggy horses carried their riders at breathtaking speeds into battle and supported them effortlessly as their mounts skirmished with sword and spear. Along with their ferocious looks, the men would yell with bloodcurdling screams and terrify their victims when engaging in battle. The animal skins which they wrapped around their shoulders also contributed to their fearsome appearance.

 Attila the Hun led his troops into battle and terrorized those they met—not least of all due to their appearance, which Westerners were not used to seeing. To them, the Huns seemed like a swarm of demons, less human than animal.

The most fiendish-looking of the warriors, Attila, king of the Huns, led his army with bold confidence. As he rode his black beast out in front, his warriors watched his every move. A confident determination showed in the thrust of his jaw, and Attila motioned to his men to charge full speed ahead.

The Huns had begun to wage their second attack on the East Roman Empire in the spring of 447 A.D., and Constantinople loomed ahead. Attila had chosen his time carefully.

Attila's possible motivation for the attack went back some years earlier—to 422 A.D. when his uncle, King Rugila, ruled the Hun kingdom. Even at that time, the Huns looked for ways to increase their land and their power. They were not an agricultural society but made their living through plundering and pillaging—that is, they conquered other peoples and took their goods, food, and possessions.

When Attila's uncle, King Rugila, discovered that the Imperial Roman Army had left just a small number of soldiers at their post on the lower Danube River, he planned to launch an attack on the Roman outpost. The condtions were right, Rugila decided, because the main force of the Roman army had left to attend to a threat from Persia.

Everything went as King Rugila planned, and after being victorious over the Roman post, he ordered his warriors on to Thrace, which was south of the Danube. Once the Huns reached Thrace, however, the government of Theodosius II struck a deal with Rugila. Theodosius II (and his government) offered a peace settlement with the Huns, and in exchange, the Romans were to pay the Huns an annual tribute of 350 pounds of gold. The Huns agreed to keep peace with the people of Thrace and its capitol, Constantinople.

An additional treaty was negotiated in 433 between the two peoples. This time, the Huns supplied soldiers to help the Roman leader Aetius, a former hostage of the Huns who had become one of the most powerful men in the Roman government. In exchange for their help, Aetius gave the Huns a part of Pannonia, known as Pannonia Secunda. King Rugila and his people were overjoyed with this new situation. For the first time, they had some permanent land. The nomadic people became more agrarian as a result.

In 434, however, King Rugila died, and his nephews Bleda and Attila became joint rulers of the Huns. Since Bleda was the eldest, he had more power than his younger brother, Attila. When the government of Constantinople decided to stop paying the Huns their annual amount of gold following Rugila's death, Bleda demanded a meeting with their representatives. The meeting took place near Margus, on the Morava River, in 435. The outcome of the treaty agreement increased the annual tribute to the Huns from 350 pounds of gold to 700. The Romans also agreed not to enter into any alliances with enemies of the Huns and to break any that already existed. Other parts of the agreement included establishing a free market on the banks of the Danube River and the release of Hun prisoners held by the Roman government.

Some years later, in 440, when Bleda and Attila breached the Treaty of Margus by attacking Castra Constantias, a Roman fortress on the Danube River, and plundering the marketplace, the Romans were angry. Bleda and Attila justified their actions by accusing the Romans of robbing Hun graves with the Bishop of Margus as an accomplice. Much treasure could be found in the graves of Hun kings, and the accusation turned out to be true. The Huns' demands were the return of fugitive Huns and the surrender of the Bishop of Margus. Neither condition was met, so the Huns took military action. The following military campaign was primarily Bleda's, with Attila playing a minor role. After the Hun army captured much territory in the Balkan Peninsula, the East Roman government negotiated a new treaty with them. The treaty again included the returning of Hun fugitives and paying any back payments in gold.

When Bleda died in 443, Attila became king of the Huns. He continued the Hun policy of finding "loopholes" in the peace treaty with the Romans and thus received an ever-increasing annual tribute of gold. Whatever Attila's reasons in 447 for his invasion of the Balkans is unclear, but this attack on the Balkans was a far greater attack than the one during Bleda's campaign in 441. In addition, the Huns' continuous need for plunder was a social necessity under Attila's leadership.

Adding to his advantage, Attila had greatly increased his army with some of the people he had conquered. Among other groups fighting with the Huns were the Gepids, led by their king, Ardaric, and the Goths, under the leadership of Valamer. Attila directed his attack through the provinces of Lower Scythia and Moesia, areas that were farther to the east than the one he conquered in 441. He planned to bypass the recent fortifications built by Nomus to protect the city of Constantinople and its suburbs.

Nomus, a master of the offices and a trusted minister of Emperor Theodosius, had received a commission from the emperor after Attila's first attack to strengthen the exposed frontier along the Danube River. In addition, the emperor ordered Nomus to bring military men stationed at the post up to their fullest potential.

When Attila and his men prepared to launch their offensive, however, a series of earthquakes erupted in the region. Beginning on January 26, 447, the quakes lasted for nearly four months and were considered to be the worst in the area's history. Like a ravenous beast, the earth opened up and devoured entire villages, and untold disasters occurred on land and sea.

Then, a few days after the earthquakes began, rain poured from the sky in rivers, according to ancient historians. So complete was the devastation from the earthquakes and water that entire hillsides were flattened, and in Constantinople, numerous buildings crumbled. In addition, countless people died as a result of the earthquakes and the plagues that followed. Of greater concern than the buildings was a stretch of the massive walls surrounding the city of Constantinople

 Constantinople was the capitol of Thrace, and the Huns had entered into an agreement with Theodosius II pledging not to attack Thrace in exchange for 350 pounds of gold every year. Luckily, its walls were fortified following an earthquake, and when the Huns broke their agreement, they bypassed the city in favor of more vulnerable ones.

that had fallen down. In an amazing turn of events, however, the men of the city began almost at once to repair the walls. Within sixty days following the earthquakes, the walls stood in place once more. This time, three tiers of walls replaced the former one, forming a barricade approximately 200 feet thick and over 100 feet high.

Meanwhile, Attila and his warriors fought the East Roman Army in battle near Marcianople and the river Utus, also known as the Vid River. The German Arnegisclus headed up the enemy army, and if anyone was up to the task of facing the invincible Attila, it was Arnegisclus. The two leaders had squared off before in the battle of 443 in the same area, and the East Roman Army had lost. Nevertheless, the brave general had learned more of Attila's battle tactics since then, so now he and his men fought confidently. But the Hun strategy of darting in and out with their small, swift horses made them difficult targets to hit. When Arnegisclus' horse was shot out from under him, he was gravely wounded and died on the battlefield. Ultimately, the Huns won the battle, but their losses were considerable.

Much of the Huns' success in battle lay in their ability as horse warriors. As nomads, they constantly traveled on horseback for hundreds of miles in the plains of Eurasia. To control their herds of cattle and sheep, they had developed their horsemanship skills, which even employed the lasso to deadly effect. A Roman officer, Ammianus, remembers the Huns' prowess with the lasso: "While the enemy are guarding against wounds from sword-thrusts, the Huns throw strips of cloth plaited into nooses over their opponents so that they are entangled and unable to ride or walk." Similar to American cowboys, the Huns walked with a bowlegged gait because of the time spent on their horses.

The Huns carried out nearly every activity on horseback. At times, they sat sidesaddle to perform certain tasks. If they had to dismount in battle, they considered themselves dead. In addition, the horses the Huns rode were rugged, shaggy ponies with short legs; the ponies were muscular and possessed great stamina. Their size offered the Huns a great deal of control over them. Further, the ponies' size also gave the

Hun archers an anchor from which to shoot, and aided them in hand-to-hand fighting.

The Huns possessed another advantage in battle: their use of the composite bow. This bow was considered the most deadly missile weapon in the ancient and medieval worlds. Archers could shoot this bow further than the customary longbow and were able to penetrate armor at 100 yards away. The Huns valued it to the extent that they presented each other bows as signs of authority. The composite bow achieved its power by the combined strength of various materials. Starting with a wooden core, the Huns next applied layers of sinew on the outside, and strips of horn on the inside. These materials were pressed together with animal glue. Usually, the horn was glued to the wood during the winter months so the setting would have a longer time to harden. Several more months of conditioning finished preparing the bow for use. The combination of wood, sinew, and horn made for a highly flexible bow and thus became perfect to use on horseback.

To Attila and his army's glee, the city of Marcianople fell. This city was the capital of Moesia Secunda and the largest city in Thrace. Attila decided not to go up against Constantinople because of its newly built protective walls; the arrows of the Huns would have merely bounced off of them. Since the Huns were not yet skilled in the use of battering rams, they had little recourse but to look elsewhere for places to conquer. Thus the city of Constantinople was spared destruction by the Huns.

As a result, Attila led his men down the Balkan peninsula. The Huns thundered on toward Greece, which awarded them another victory, but they were stopped at Thermopylae. The Huns destroyed everything in their pathway and plundered the rest. Utter devastation of each place resulted and countless people were slaughtered. A man by the name of Callinicus captured the brutality of

Not only were the Huns skilled archers on horseback, but they used the lasso as a combat weapon to great effect. A Roman officer recalled, "While the enemy are guarding against wounds from sword-thrusts, the Huns throw strips of cloth plaited into nooses over their opponents so that they are entangled and unable to ride or walk."

this campaign when he wrote of the "barbarian nation of the Huns":

> which was in Thrace, became so great that more than a hundred cities were captured and Constantinople almost came into danger and most men fled from it. . . . And there were so many murders and blood-lettings that the dead could not be numbered. Ay, for they took the churches and monasteries and slew the monks and maidens in great numbers.

A final assessment of the carnage as given by Count Marcellinus some years later was that "Attila ground almost the whole of Europe into the dust."

THE RISE
OF THE HUNS

Sweeping winds of change began to blow through eastern Europe and beyond in the fourth and fifth centuries. The land and the people alike experienced continuous upheaval as hordes of warriors known as barbarians destroyed their homes and their way of life.

One of these barbaric groups, the Huns (known to the Chinese as the *Hsiung-nu*) fought their way west from the Chinese border. They had already battled with the Chinese to the extent that the Chinese lavished tribute on them in the form of gold, silk, and female slaves. Historian Edward Gibbon remarked that "A select band of the fairest maidens of China was annually devoted to the rude embraces of the Huns."

The Chinese were so fearful of these marauding warriors that they constructed the Great Wall of China to protect themselves against them. Construction of the 2500-mile wall was begun in 221 B.C. and extended across northern China from the Yellow Sea to the Cental Asian desert. The ruler, Qin Shihuangdi, along with

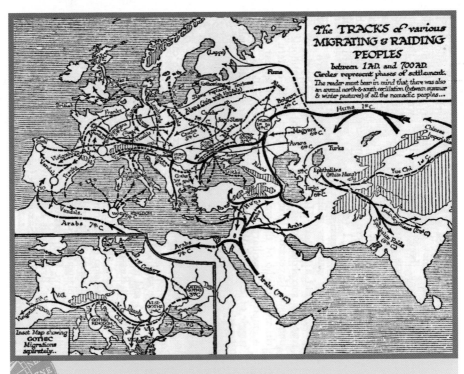

This map shows the various migrating patterns of people of the ancient world, including the Huns. By the time Attila was born, the Huns' empire stretched into modern-day Russia, Hungary, and China.

300,000 of his troops, began work on the wall to which later Chinese dynasties added 600 more miles. The wall was twenty-five feet high and twelve feet wide; the builders constructed it of earth and stone with a brick facing.

Later on, when the Huns had migrated to Central Europe, they continued to have some connections with the Chinese. When the Chinese emperor Wu-Ti opened the western Silk Road trade route, groups of six and ten Hun families would travel together on the road en route to and from China. Each Hun family unit would also have a feeding area for their animals.

In their westward trek, the Huns settled along the banks of the Tisza River in an area today known as Hungary. The Tisza River flows north and south, somewhat parallel to the Danube

River in this same area. The Tisza, near the present-day south-eastern Hungarian city of Szeged, is wide and impressive. The countryside here, except for a few small hills, is flat. This land is known as the Hortobagy; horses are plentiful here, and other animals include sheep with twisted horns and herds of buffaloes. Several varieties of birds such as curlews, larks, bustards, barriers, and white storks are also numerous.

By the fifth century, the Huns controlled an empire that reached from the Ural Mountains of Russia to the Rhone River in Central and Southwestern Europe from the plain area of Hungary. Here, in 406 A.D., Attila was born. Attila's father was King Mundzuk, and Attila had at least one older brother whose name was Bleda. Attila, being the son of a king, enjoyed many royal privileges. But he was not pampered. Instead, at an early age, he became disciplined and taught to endure many hardships—even not having enough to eat. Like other young Hun boys, he also learned how to hunt and ride horseback.

At the age of eight, Attila organized war games with his playmates. He and his friends relished riding their ponies into mock battles in which they used toy swords and bows and arrows. Attila's group usually won these games, but the mock battles the children fought were all too fierce and realistic. Many of the leadership qualities Attila displayed later as an adult developed as a result of these games.

Since the Huns were a nomadic people, their herds supplied most of their food and clothing. Such a meager food supply afforded the Huns a meager existence—with nothing wasted. Their clothing, too, consisted of just the barest essentials—linen and animal skins sewn together. The Huns would wear their clothing until it wore out.

Attila, like his early childhood friends, grew accustomed to being hungry and thirsty—at times because there was simply nothing to eat. In spite of these hardships, Attila grew strong and vigorous. The ponies he and his friends rode were known as "steppe" ponies (steppes are plains). The adults rode these ponies as well, and since the ponies were small, like the riders, each suited the other well.

The Romans thought the Huns lived on horseback since the horse and the rider were so attuned to each other: "They are unable to put their feet firmly on the ground: they live and sleep on their horses," notes Zosimus. The Huns' appearance also worked to their advantage, as their enemies—especially the Romans—found them repulsive to look at, and said they could not be sure whether the Huns were men or animals.

A Roman veterinary surgeon, Vegetius Renatus, describes the Huns' horses:

> The Hunnish horses have large heads, curved like hooks, protruding eyes, narrow nostrils, broad jaws, strong and rigid necks. Their manes hang down to their knees, their ribs are big, their backbones curved, and their tails shaggy. They have very strong shinbones and small feet, their hooves being full and broad, and the soft parts hollow.

Renatus goes on to note that the Hun horses' bodies were angular and without fat on their rumps or "protruberances" on the muscles. In addition, he writes, "The stature is rather long than tall. The trunk is vaulted, and the bones are strong, and the leanness of the horses is striking. But one forgets the ugly appearance of these horses as this is set off by their fine qualities: their sober nature, cleverness and their ability to endure any injuries very well."

Similar to other nomadic peoples, the Huns were ruled in time of war by their leading warriors. Most likely their prowess in war helped these men—like Attila's father, King Mundzuk—to achieve their leading positions. In the rare times of peace, however, all the men took turns looking after the animals and seeking fresh pasture for them.

In fact, one of the main reasons the Huns moved westward was because of the arid climate cycle that currently prevailed over Eastern Europe. These cycles would last several hundred

Two Mongolian horseman from the 1950s pose on their horses. The horses have changed little over the years since Attila's time, and to the Romans, these small creatures were unique and previously unseen until the Huns came westward.

years until a less arid cycle began. At the same time the drier climate cycle occurred, the temperature turned several degrees cooler. The coinciding of these two changes jeopardized the Huns' grazing areas. Consequently, they sought greener pastures for their herds further west.

The Huns had extensive herds consisting of cattle, horses, goats, and sheep. Since they were not an agricultural society at this time, their food supply came not only from their herds, but also from hunting. Attila loved the excitement of the hunt. To prepare, he spent many hours a day practicing with his bow and arrow. Rarely did he need to use two arrows for his prey. Most of the time, his arrows went straight to the mark— whether it was bullseye or animal.

Of course, Attila and his other friends also had their share of chores to do. The animals had to be looked after, the cows needed milking, and sometimes, Attila would have to shear the sheep. Since the Huns traded products like wool and animal skins, Attila tried to pay close attention to his father's instruction as he guided the sharp knife over a sheep's body so as not to cut the animal.

Another chore that Attila disliked to some extent was making sure his family's tent was strong and without holes through which the rain and snow could penetrate. To Attila, this job was somewhat monotonous, but nevertheless, he tried to do his best. He knew his father was depending on him; and whatever he did, he wanted his father to be proud of him.

Attila's "family" actually consisted of six to ten families who joined themselves together to make up a clan. In addition, in times of war, numerous clans grouped themselves together to form a tribe. The entire Hun society was made up of loosely joined groups that were similar to Attila's.

By the time of Attila's eleventh birthday, Roman soldiers invaded the Huns' camp. The Hun men fought bravely, killing and wounding a number of soldiers, but they were caught off guard. The result was disastrous: the Hun camp was in shambles, and King Mundzuk lay dead. Following the battle, the two factions declared a truce, but also negotiated a hostage-treaty agreement. Attila was to be one of the hostages. He would go to the Roman court of Emperor Honorius at Ravenna, Italy, and would remain there through his teenage years.

Saddened by his father's death, Attila nevertheless felt little fear about his journey to the Roman capital of Ravenna. Of course, he would miss his family and friends, especially his Uncle Rugila and good friend Oldo. But he remembered the ancient prophecy about the magical sword of the war god. The one the gods favored would discover it—and a seer had told Attila that he was the chosen one. This prophecy, hidden in his heart, gave the young Attila hope for the days ahead.

3

AT THE COURT
OF HONORIUS

The Romans had only given Attila time to get his beloved bow and a small knapsack in which he put some treasured mementoes. Now, with each twist and turn of the dusty road, Attila's eyes took in new sights. After many days and nights on the road crossing mountains and traveling around huge bodies of water, the men and their animals were becoming much fatigued. By the time they started seeing small, scattered villages along the Italian coast, they knew they would soon reach Ravenna.

A brisk wind blew off the Adriatic Sea as the company arrived at their destination. Ravenna was the capital of the Western Roman Empire while Constantinople was the capital of the Eastern Roman Empire. Ravenna had been designated the new capital of the empire in 402 A.D., just prior to the fall of Rome. Alaric and his Visigoth army captured and sacked the city of Rome a few years later in 410 A.D. Reflecting on the catastrophe, St. Jerome (Church Father and author

Honorius, shown here feeding birds, was the emperor of Rome when Attila was brought to Ravenna. He and his court would introduce Attila to the Roman lifestyle, which was completely different from the Huns' nomadic one.

of the Latin Vulgate Bible) remarked: "When the brightest light of the whole earth was extinguished, when the Roman Empire was deprived of its head, when the whole world perished in one city, then I was dumb with silence, I held my peace even from God, and my sorrow was stirred."

By that time, the emperor and the government had been

safely established at Ravenna, on the Adriatic shore, so the actual fall of Rome had little military significance. Because it was surrounded by marshes and water and was thus fairly impregnable, Ravenna was a good choice for the capital. The city also boasted a healthful climate.

Shortly after Attila's arrival in Ravenna, one of Honorius' attendants showed him his quarters and the bath area. Attila was amazed; he had never seen a bath! In addition, the attendant laid out clean clothing and set out fresh fruit. Since Attila didn't yet speak Latin, and the attendant couldn't speak the Hunnish language, the two had some difficulty understanding each other. Nevertheless, Attila tried to let the man know he appreciated the kindness shown him. Attila, not quite twelve, wondered about the person in charge of all this wealth. Soon after he had refreshed himself, he would meet Honorius, the emperor of the Western Roman Empire.

Honorius himself had been Attila's age when he became emperor in 395 A.D. following the death of his father, Theodosius I. His brother, Arcadius, became emperor of the Eastern Roman Empire at Constantinople at just seventeen. Because of Honorius' youth, however, he had an appointed guardian by the name of Stilicho. By birth, Stilicho was from the Vandals, one of the barbaric tribes that swept across Europe in the fourth and fifth centuries. A powerful, dynamic man, Stilicho sought to preserve the western empire. In 401, the barbarian Visigoths invaded Italy in search of new homelands and besieged Milan, Italy. However, by 402, Stilicho, with help from the tribes of Alans and Vandals, was able to drive the Visigoths back. Later on, after making an arrangement with Alaric, the Visigoth leader, for various unused military services, Stilicho managed to indebt himself to Alaric. Alaric demanded payment but was refused, after which he invaded Italy again in 408. Because of Stilicho's alleged misdeeds, Honorius had him executed. Now, at twenty-three, Honorius ruled the Western Roman Empire alone.

As Attila, now a kind of exchange student, began to get used to his civilized surroundings, he began to enjoy himself. He even attended some classes, including ones in Latin, where he learned to speak and understand more of the Romans' language. Life in Ravenna was very different from his life with the Huns living near the Tisza River. He actually missed riding his pony, doing chores, and hunting. Life here was too easy, Attila decided. In spite of the ease, he determined to get as much as he could from his time at Ravenna.

Attila received pleasure from going to the Roman Circus where there were acrobats, jugglers, and other kinds of acts. He had never seen anything like the skill of these performers. Honorius did spend some time with Attila, but he was usually too busy to talk much with him. But now that Attila had learned some Latin, they could converse more. When Honorius did talk with him, though, he asked Attila many questions about the Huns. He thought maybe Attila would divulge some of the Huns' future plans, but Attila usually did not say much, possessing a reserved temperament.

Although Attila didn't see much of Honorius in the daytime, he did see him some in the evenings. Many nights, dinner consisted of a lavish feast with an abundance of meat, fish, fowl, vegetables, fruits, and breads of all types, and sumptuous desserts—even ice cream, which Attila particularly enjoyed. Runners obtained the ice in the mountains and brought it all the way to the city where chefs quickly mixed it with other ingredients to make this early form of ice cream. Attila admitted in halting Latin to Honorius that the Roman meals had much more variety that the Hunnish ones. The one aspect of dining Roman-style that Attila disliked, however, was reclining to eat meals. The Huns generally sat to eat their meals—many times on horseback.

Honorius became most helpful to Attila. He taught him much about Roman history. Honorius attempted to tell Attila quite a lot about the different emperors who had ruled Rome—

The typical Roman way to eat was while reclining—something Attila did not find to his liking. But he did admit that the Romans had a much wider variety of food with their meals than the Huns did. In fact, Attila became quite fond of ice cream, which in those days was made with ice from the mountains.

but the city and the empire had existed so long, he found it difficult to include everyone.

As the empire grew, Rome needed more and more men for the army. Attila was most interested in the Roman army. He had heard stories around the campfire about the prowess of Roman soldiers. He heard, too, that all their armor slowed them down in contrast to the Huns, who generally wore animal skins to their battles. For many centuries, the Roman army served as a peacekeeping force on its far-flung frontiers. In the fourth and fifth centuries, with the movement of many peoples like the Goths, Visigoths, Vandals, and Huns, the frontiers became more and more threatened, requiring an ever increasing number of men in the army.

As time passed and Attila entered his teens, he became more intrigued with Roman life in Ravenna. He learned that each Roman town had certain public buildings for all the populace to enjoy. These buildings included an amphitheater, a theater, circus, forum, and temples along with other amenities and structures such as aqueducts, sewers, latrines, and, of course, public bathhouses. Many towns also built defensive city walls and monumental arches, and gates to the city. Usually, these arches commemorated some mark of civic pride, the foundation of the town, or the exploits of the retired soldiers who lived there. The forum housed the town's civic center and had administration and trade rooms as well as areas used for meeting rooms.

The public baths in each Roman town often provided a center for the town's social life. Attila frequently made the effort to visit the baths on a daily basis, as he enjoyed soaking in the water and listening to the daily gossip—which he could make out fairly well by this time with his greatly improved Latin.

Attila also became curious about the Romans' religion. Their religion and form of worship appeared to be very different from that of the Huns. He asked Honorius, "Tell me about your religion and your gods." Honorius took Attila on a tour of various temples in the city of Ravenna. He also told him, "We Romans worship many different gods." Some of the main gods of the Romans were Jupiter, Juno and Minerva. The Romans compared the Greek god Zeus with the Roman god, Jupiter, who became father and king of the gods. Thus, Jupiter's wife, Juno, became queen of the gods. Juno was identified with the Greek goddess Hera, and was also the goddess of marriage and women. Minerva, who was similar to the Greek goddess Athena, was the goddess of war and of wisdom.

Of course, the Romans had many, many other lesser deities, and a good number of Roman citizens by the time of Theodosius I had embraced Christianity. In fact, Theodosius I had himself become a Christian and closed many of the pagan temples. At the close of the fourth century, Theodosius abolished all pagan sacrifices and seized the temple estates, but he allowed the traditional games and festivals to continue.

Attila was curious about the Romans' religion, and asked Flavius to enlighten him. Honorius showed him the various temples and told him of the different gods that they worshipped. This was another aspect that was quite different from the Huns' religion, which employed shamans and worshipped nature gods.

The Huns, on the other hand, worshipped nature deities, looked to seers and *shamans* (priests who practice magic to cure the sick or divine the future), and used a practice known as *scapulimancy*. Scapulimancy was the Huns' method of fore-telling future events by carefully looking at cattle entrails as well as at certain streaks in bone scrapings.

Startled by the great differences in the Romans' and the Huns' religion, Attila suddenly became homesick. But there were many other differences in the two societies as well. By this time he had been at the court of Honorius for a number of years and had grown into a young man. He was homesick for his own people and his own culture. When he spoke to Honorius about returning to his own people, Honorius told him to go in peace. Honorius gave him provision for his journey and a number of thoughtful gifts. So, Attila left the city of Ravenna and the court of Honorius with much joy in his heart: after many days, he would see his own people again.

ATTILA'S RETURN

Attila had at last arrived back in the Hun camp on the Hungarian plain. He was so happy to see everyone, especially his uncle, King Rugila, and his brother Bleda. Everyone and everything looked so different. But he had changed a lot, too. He had grown into a young man while he had been at Ravenna. He had changed so much, in fact, that even his closest friends and family members scarcely recognized him.

One person Attila met for the first time in the Hun camp was a half-German, half-Roman teenager who was a child hostage like himself. The young man's name was Aetius, and he had been with the Huns about the same length of time Attila had been at Honorius' court. Attila enjoyed meeting Aetius, as the two seemed to have a lot in common. However, Aetius planned to leave the same day as Attila's next trip—but fate would bring the two together again.

Upon his return to the Huns, Attila decided to become an ambassador and try to unite the various Hun tribes into an army. Attila drew upon his experiences in Ravenna to motivate the tribes he addressed, and the Huns entertained his thoughts with great enthusiasm, dreaming of the land and riches they could win as one people.

After spending a brief time at home, Attila grew restless. He conferred with his uncle about traveling throughout the huge Hun territory as a goodwill ambassador, as well as attempting to unify the diverse Hun tribes. His uncle liked the idea, and

Attila set out the following day on his new venture.

The first place Attila's travels took him was to the north-ernmost part of the Hun kingdom in present-day Germany. Attila realized from his time with the Romans in Ravenna that the Huns needed to come together in unity for greater power and conquest. As the situation existed now, the tribes were isolated and separated from each other. When he met with the various Hunnic leaders on his travels, he tried to persuade them to give up some of their personal power to a central government to achieve greater strength. Thus, in the evenings around a campfire, the leaders gave Attila permission to speak.

So, Attila began: "During my childhood, when our nation was ruled by my father and his brothers, they often sold the services of their warriors to the Romans." However, said Attila, too many times Hun soldiers have laid down their lives for alien governments—and without bettering themselves or their own country. Unfortunately, "Our ancestors could only see their present goals, so they willingly accepted campaign missions from the Romans." Attila admitted that at first, "I did, too. But I see now that I was wrong."

The Hun leaders and their tribes in the north liked what Attila had to say. They begged him to stay on awhile and to continue giving them his insights. Attila's superior education in the Roman court stood him well. Not only did he learn to speak Latin, the Roman language, but he learned a great deal about the Roman way of life—as well as information about their military strategies. He knew the once-powerful Roman army now was forced to hire men from barbaric tribes to defend their homeland frontiers and their way of life.

Although the Huns' reputation of being fierce warriors and primitive nomads was true to some extent, the fact that their ragtag army could challenge the crumbling Western Roman Empire at the Danube River proved that they were more than mere savages. The Romans, of course, spread bleak tales of the Huns' cruelty—but the Romans could be cruel to their enemies too.

The Huns' tribal arrangement proved to be their main obstacle to accomplishing more in battle. A warrior-chieftan led each tribe; further, each of these chiefs acted independently from any other groups. As they wandered from place to place, however, the various groups intermarried with other peoples like the Mongols, the Germans, and the Scandinavians. One tribe that retained its Mongol characteristics formed the Huns' aristocracy.

Now it was Attila's task to motivate each of these tribal chieftans to catch a vision of a greater empire for the Huns than they had ever imagined. When the Huns gathered around the campfire at night, they leaned forward eagerly to hear Attila speak. Again, he spoke of the good to be gained from establishing a common goal through unity: "If we are to break the shackles of poverty and escape our nomadic way of life, we must unite our tribes in a strong Hunnic confederacy. This will not be easy. All Huns must be convinced that more is to be gained by working together than by fighting one another or by fighting the Romans." Attila followed his central theme with a challenge to each leader. He said that each of them needed to involve each of their warriors in the cause—to help each warrior to catch the vision of a united Hunnic empire, and to tell these men what it could mean to them and their families to have a unified government and how their way of life could be improved.

The time Attila spent in Ravenna as a child hostage continued to serve him well as he told the various Hun groups about something he had witnessed at court. He told them about the greed of the eunuchs and ministers who took care of the tax collection. Attila realized that of all the taxes collected, only a small amount ever made it to the imperial treasury. In addition, he told the Huns, "Corrupt officials used the Empire's money to buy powerful positions in

As nomads, the Huns' tribal arrangement had previously prevented them from consolidating their resources and assembling an army worthy of taking on the Roman army. Attila's greatest challenge was to convince tribal chiefs of the benefits of fighting together with other tribes rather than looking out for their own tribes' interests.

Honorius' court. And they paid no taxes on their ill-gotten personal fortunes, while the Roman people were burdened by overtaxation." Attila could scarcely contain his disgust at what he witnessed at the court; he determined then and there that corruption must not be allowed among the Huns. No greedy tribal chieftan would be allowed to abuse the booty— all would share and share alike.

Attila continued on his travels, going to the eastern edge of the Huns' territory toward Russia and China, then south toward the Hungarian plains, and finally eastward toward Italy and France. He spoke to groups of Huns everywhere he went, praising them for past victories, yet urging them to come together for greater triumphs and rewards. Everywhere he went, the Huns received him enthusiastically. Attila could speak forcefully, yet he maintained a humble demeanor. For years he travelled among the Huns, paving the way for the kingdom that was to come under his leadership as he created goodwill, unity, and above all, a new vision.

ATTILA AND BLEDA SHARE THE THRONE

Attila's time after being gone several years was now marked by sadness but also excitement. His Uncle Rugila died in 433 — and Attila and Bleda were now co-rulers of the Hun kingdom. Attila would miss his elderly uncle. He had guided the Huns for many years and had much wisdom. However, Attila sensed the time was drawing near to implement his vision for the Huns.

Even though Bleda and Attila were now co-rulers, Attila was undoubtedly considered second in command due to his age. Since Bleda established his headquarters in the lower Tisza River area, he let it be known that he was the supreme commander. Attila's domain existed further down the Danube in the Bucharest-Ploesti region.

In the meantime, Bleda and Attila had another situation at hand. After their Uncle Rugila's death, the government in Constantinople chose to ignore a treaty it had reached with the Huns earlier. Bleda called their bluff, and through a serious of shrewd maneuvers, he and

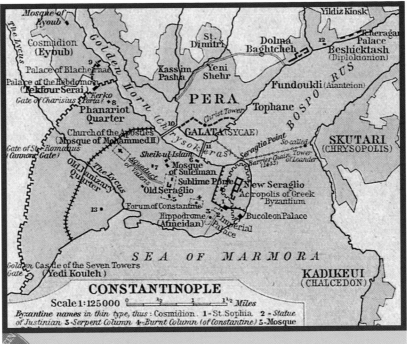

Once Bleda and Attila became rulers of the Huns, they had to deal with the problem of Constantinople reneging on their previous deal with the Huns. The two brothers were able to get the government in Constantinope to enter into the Treaty of Margus with the Huns—one of their first major (and bloodless) victories.

Attila not only got the original treaty terms reinstated, but additional ones besides. So, the Treaty of Margus in 435 proved to be a triumph for the young Hun rulers.

By 439 and 440, the Roman Empire faced wars on several fronts. The Vandals raided Carthage in what is now North Africa in 439. Earlier, the city had been completely destroyed by the Roman Republican forces, but once more had become a city of major importance. The following year, both the Eastern and Western Empires sent armies to ward off the Vandals and thus defend Sicily. At the same time, the Persians attacked Armenia.

As he heard of these various attacks, Bleda became convinced that he had another opportunity to plunder the Balkans. Bleda planned his campaign in two stages. First, a limited operation would result in the capture of Viminiacum (now the Serbian town of Kostolac). Following this battle, there would be a brief truce. However, the war began anew the next year in 441. The Huns planned to capture the city of Margus, which was taken most easily. The Bishop of Margus realized that it would be far wiser to allow the Huns to enter the city peacefully than to have them destroy the city, so after bargaining for his own freedom, he apparently even opened the city's gates for the Huns himself.

Afterward the Huns moved southward with little opposition. Soon, they captured Constantine's birthplace, a town called Nish (or Naissus). Other towns they captured were Sofia (Serdica) and Plovdiv (Philoppolis). The Huns were not able to take all of the fortresses, however, like Edirne (Hadrianople) and Iregli (Heracleia). Nevertheless, the Huns reached the sea at three points: at Callipolis; at Sestus, south of the capital; and an unspecified place north of it.

Their way now clear to the capital, the Huns raced down the military highway which ran along the Hebrus Valley. By the time they conquered Philippopolis, there was no longer anything standing in their way. The ancient city of Philippopolis was the crossroads of the well-traveled north-south road from Oescus on the Danube to the Aegean Sea and also the highway running from the Bosphorus to the West. While Edirne and Iregli were either passed over by the Huns or were able to ward them off, Arcadiopolis was taken. The Huns gained much booty from their attack, and the prisoners they took could not even be fully counted.

The new army of Theodosius finally met up with the Hun army. Theodosius' army was commanded by Aspar, an Alan who had negotiated an earlier truce, and by Arnegisclus. These two men were probably two of the Roman army's foremost generals, but proved no match for Attila. Theodosius' army fought the Huns in a series of battles outside the capital but suffered heavy defeats in each. Finally, in a swift maneuver, the Huns cut off the Romans from Constantinople and forced them back to the Chersonesus. The Huns also controlled a fortress just outside the city walls. Since the Huns were not equipped to attack the thick city walls of Constantinople, Attila turned on General Aspar's army in the Chersonesus. In one last battle, he rendered a tremendous defeat to the Roman forces.

The Empire could take credit for just one success—and one that did not involve the regular army. A large contingent of Huns, led by some of their outstanding commanders, had been sent to invade Lower Moesia. These warriors had already made off with much booty and numerous captives just before arriving at the small but powerful town of Asemus. The town was situated on the frontier between Oescus and Ad Novas. Here, the small river Asemus (modern Osma) flows into the Danube nine miles east of the Utus (Vid). The town's citizens took matters into their own hands instead of merely relying on their strong city walls or outside moat. The Huns, weighed down by their booty and many captives, were caught off guard when the men of Asemus fell upon them. Many Huns died in the onslaught, even though the men of Asemus were outnumbered, and the men in turn rescued the Roman prisoners.

However, the victory at Asemus was a small one compared to the defeat of the Romans at Chersonesus. Theodosius had no choice but to ask for merciful terms. This time, the Supreme Commander of the Eastern Army and Consul-Senator Anatolius carried out the treaty negotiations with the Huns. First, the Huns wanted the Hun prisoners given back immediately. Then, Attila insisted on payment of the gold tribute, which was in arrears, and calculated it to be 6000 pounds. He also wanted the gold tribute to be increased three times, or to 2100 pounds annually. In addition, the Romans were not to receive any Hun fugitives. A provisional treaty went into effect on August 27, 443.

Attila's clever diplomacy soon became evident as he sent ambassador after ambassador to Constantinople pressing for the

After the defeat of the Romans at Chersonesus, Attila was able to negotiate terms with the Romans that not only tripled the annual gold tribute but also freed all Hun prisoners of war. Attila would also send ambassadors to receive lavish gifts from the Romans, in effect getting booty from the Romans without having to spill a drop of blood.

return of all the Hun fugitives. Each time, Theodosius' ministers gave the ambassadors beautiful gifts—as was the custom—but maintained that no fugitives had been left on Roman soil. While this was most likely true, Attila simply sent the ambassadors so that they might receive the numerous and costly presents which the Roman government was expected to bestow. After innumerable Hun complaints, Attila's ambassadors increased their riches. The entire operation thus turned into a tremendous, and uncharacteristically nonviolent, victory for the Huns.

Soon after, Bleda died in 445. The cause of his death are uncertain, but there are various theories. One theory is that Bleda didn't have much interest in the affairs of state and left Attila to deal with them. After taking up hunting, Bleda may have died in a hunting accident. Another theory is that Attila had Bleda murdered. Although either theory could be true, it seems more likely that Bleda and Attila had a power struggle.

Not much is known about Bleda, but he and Attila did have their disagreements. One of the disagreements concerned a dwarf named Zerko. Zerko had belonged to the Imperial general Aspar. The Huns captured Zerko, and he provided Bleda with continuous amusement. Bleda even gave Zerko a Hun wife. Attila, however, did not like Zerko. When Bleda died, Attila gave the dwarf to Aetius, who then returned him to Aspar. But when Zerko wanted his Hun wife returned, Attila refused. The incident appears minor, but to contemporary chroniclers, it serves to illustrate differences between the brothers, and also points up the fact that they possibly had numerous squabbles throughout their shared reign.

One day, a herdsman became aware that one of his cows was lame. Upon closer inspection, he realized its foot had been cut. As he followed the trail of blood to its source, he located a very old sword covered up by the grass. He picked it up and took it to Attila. Whether true or not, Attila believed it fulfilled the prophecy that had been told to him many years earlier involving the sword of the war god, and that whoever should find it would be the chosen one. The Huns accepted the prophecy as well. With Bleda gone, Attila was now the undisputed king of the Huns—but now he had the divine prophecy that seemingly confirmed his destiny.

For a few years, the Huns remained at peace. One of their Roman prisoners remarked later about their idle, carefree life in peace time with "each man enjoying his present blessings and neither causing trouble nor suffering it." But before long, Attila would expand the Hun kingdom into a worldwide empire.

ATTILA'S KINGDOM

When the Roman emissaries entered Attila's throne room, they expected to see a dazzling display of gold, silver, and jewels adorning the king of the Huns. Instead, they were astonished to see Attila sitting on a rustic, wooden throne wearing a Western-style tunic that lacked embellishment of any kind. His royal position was maintained with dignity, but without ostentation and luxury. Even his palace, although the finest building in town, was simple and unadorned—totally unlike the palaces and estates of the Romans. An observer noted that even Attila's "personal habits were modest. He refused to adorn his shoes with gold and silver as many of the Hunnic noblemen did. No precious-metal mountings decorated the bows of his saddle. No jewels were embedded in the bridle worn by his magnificent war horse. He drank from a wooden cup and ate meat served on a wooden platter. His simple clothes were kept conspicuously

The Romans who visited Attila to offer tribute were surprised at how spartan his living conditions were, especially considering the treasures that the Huns received as tribute and through conquest. Indeed, Attila's throne was made of wood, and he wore no precious metals on his clothing.

clean by his personal attendants." Although he didn't insist that the Huns imitate him in his simple lifestyle, he did urge them to avoid extravagance.

The Romans themselves had come bearing some of the

annual tribute and called in their servants to present the gold to Attila. In turn, the servants trudged in with as many bags of gold coins as they could carry and carefully placed them on a prepared table. With a smile on his face, Attila stepped over to the table to begin counting the Roman offering. Then he turned and called to his secretary, Constantius, "Please see that these gentlemen have proper food and lodging after their long journey."

Constantius, an Italian, was Attila's principal secretary. Another of Attila's intimate advisors was Orestes. He came to Attila's court to offer his services and brought his wife with him. Orestes' wife's father commanded the army of the Roman province of Noricum. From the first day Orestes arrived at the court, Attila gave him a prominent position. Moreover, Romulus, Orestes' son, became the last of the Roman emperors in the West.

Another person in Attila's court who exercised considerable influence was Eudoxius, a former doctor. Attila also had two prominent brothers in his court. Although their racial origins could not be determined, their immediate background and culture was Greek and Hellenistic. The one, Onegesius, was a *vizier*, or court chamberlain, while the other, Scotta, received instructions from Attila to collect the gold and Hun fugitives.

As a leader of his people, Attila knew he had to surround himself with people who could help the Huns better them-selves—people who could teach them new ways of doing things. Thus, he selected individuals from other countries who were highly skilled in their respective areas. These men were familiar with the outside world and spoke one of the two principal languages of the day—either Latin, which was the language of the Romans and the West, or Greek, the common language of the East.

Attila represented the final, absolute authority to his people. Priscus noted that Attila "appears among his people amid the shouts of their applause; but their respect is based on fear . . . the entire multitude of the Huns was pervaded by terror of him. . . . he felt [not] the slightest limitation on his power either in war or in peace. He plans and conducts campaigns and negotiations apparently without any consultation with, or advice from, his followers." In addition, in peaceful times, Attila would wait outside his home and dispense justice to the people who come to him with their problems. These people would accept Attila's decisions without question.

Attila's advisors carried out diplomatic missions, and sometimes negotiated with foreign ambassadors who came to see Attila. Each of these individuals constituted Attila's close associates, or picked men. One of them, Edeco, belonged to the group because of his military prowess and his outstanding successes in warfare. Another confidante, Berichus, had been born into a noble family. Most likely his family in the preceding generation had distinguished themselves in the field and, in return, had obtained much wealth from plunder.

In addition, each of these men had his own military force assigned to him—but each knew to whom his loyalty belonged. Thus, each of these men and their forces ruled over different parts of the Hun empire. For example, Attila appointed Berichus to rule over many villages in Scythia, and Onegesius, Edeco, and the others undoubtedly also ruled over other villages. By sharing this power, they were almost Attila's own sons, as Attila had designated his eldest son, Ellac, to rule over the once-subdued nation of the Acatziri.

A sort of hierarchy also existed among the men, indicated by their seats when they sat down to eat at feasts. Onegesius sat at the right hand of Attila, while Berichus sat at his left. The Roman Orestes had to be satisfied with a rank much below Edeco, because Edeco was a Hun by race and the most outstanding fighter. The territories each of these men ruled over may very well have differed in size, population, wealth, and importance accordingly as well.

A further duty for these men was to collect tribute and

foodstuffs from subject nations. The Huns themselves hated agriculture and depended on other peoples for their food supply—people like the Goths, who labored as slaves to produce food for themselves and the Huns. One episode that clearly illustrates both the slave status of subject peoples and the Huns' need for food is given by Chelchal in reference to the days of Attila: "The Huns, who themselves despised agriculture, descended upon the Gothic food-supply and snatched it away like wolves, so that the Goths had the status of slaves and laboured for the sustenance of the Huns." The Huns often had to import the grain they used from other countries to feed their growing military forces. Thus, agricultural produce from a people called the Gepids included wheat, barley, rye, peas, and various forms of fruit.

Many of the people conquered by the Huns became their slaves. Although multitudes of people fled before the Huns in an attack, the ones that stayed behind became their subjects. In addition, the men were often required to fight for the Huns. As early as 375, the Huns had forced conquered peoples to fight for them. At that time, the newly conquered Alans headed up an attack on the Ostrogoths. Then, in 408, the Hun chief Uldin attacked Thrace with a number of Sciri in his army. Attila, too, usually set off on a campaign with numerous troops from his subject peoples. The subject warriors increased the numbers, but also it would have been dangerous for Attila to leave them behind when the main Hun army was away.

These close associates of Attila's helped him administer his entire empire. Berichus, for example, had ruled a number of villages in Scythia, but in 449, he left there to be with Attila in his select circle of administrators. Later, he served Attila as an ambassador to Constantinople. Berichus' ability to serve Attila implies that in this way, the military force he used to keep his part of the conquered peoples in check was considerable: he could not have allowed himself to be gone unless he felt assured

Attila knew he could not rule over his empire alone. He made sure that conquered peoples would also fight for the Hun army, and that the leaders of subject peoples would remain in place as leaders who would have to answer ultimately to Attila.

of the safety of his troops and their wives and children. So, his military forces must have been such that they could keep at bay the subject peoples' bitter hostility from hungrily witnessing their grain taken away each year to nourish their masters.

On the other hand, the Huns needed certain leaders of the subject peoples to rule their own people, since their empire was so extensive. These leaders still had to answer to Attila. Two of these subject leaders were Ardaric, king of the Gepid people, and Valamer, the elder king of the Ostrogoths. Each of these men appear to have been on par with Attila's inner circle of confidantes. Ardaric's favored position, for example, meant that no enemy outside or inside the Hun camp could strike against him to any extent so long as Attila remained his friend.

Most of the minor princes, chieftains, and leaders of various nations enjoyed little favor. In fact, Jordanes observed that "[They] hung upon Attila's nod like slaves, and when he gave a sign even by a glance without a murmur, each stood up in fear and trembling, and without hesitation did as he was ordered."

Polygamy was practiced throughout Hun society, and the rulers had a number of wives. The first wife received precedence over the others, and her children also were the most favored. But the lot of women was not as bleak as first appears. On one occasion, Attila rode into his chief village, and the Hun women came running up from all sides to catch a glimpse of him, even singing songs of welcome to him. When Attila had travelled a little farther down the road, Onegesius' wife came from her hut with several of her handmaidens, offering food and drink to Attila. He accepted the gifts graciously, wanting to please his lieutenant's wife. Here, the Hun women are allowed to appear in public and mix with the throng—not only with their own male relatives, but also with strangers and foreigners.

Evidently, on occasion, women could be tribal leaders. Bleda's widow, for example, ruled her village, and she may have ruled other villages in the area as well. Although other women rulers do not appear among the Huns themselves, a tribe called the Utiguri, which had a nation much like that of the

Huns, had at least one female tribal leader. In addition, in Justinian's time, the Sabiri, who were considered to be Huns, had a woman leader called Boarex, who had assumed the command of her tribe when her husband, Balach, died. Thus, women in Attila's kingdom may have held fairly high positions of dignity and respect not expected of a "barbaric" people.

By Attila's time, the Hun economy had shifted from being a pastoral economy with flocks and herds to a more monetary system. Attila cultivated his followers by providing money and material possessions for them, rewarding his chieftains with the best of the booty they acquired. In addition to gaining booty by plunder, Attila would send embassies on to Constantinople and other places and obtain booty by diplomacy. Thus his inner circle of men received gifts of silk and Indian pearls, gold and silver platters, silver goblets and trays, bridles studded with gold and precious stones, beds covered with linen, and other fineries.

The elite group also enjoyed food such as dates, Indian pepper, delicacies, and other items. Earlier in their society, the Huns had only eaten meat on special occasions, or perhaps at a feast of some visiting dignitary. Now, meat became a regular feature of the ruling class' meals. They also had wine to drink regularly—along with several varieties of Germanic beer. An East Roman dignitary wrote of one of Attila's feasts, calling it "a sumptuous dinner. It began about the ninth hour and went on all night. There were tables, chairs, and couches of the Roman fashion. The Roman influence is very clear in the arrangement of the tables, each of which was set before three or four of the guests."

Even the large huts of Attila and Onegesius show the considerable difference between Attila's Huns and those of earlier times whose homes were horse-drawn wagons. However, the limited Hun economy could not have produced most of these possessions and luxuries. Neither did the majority of Attila's followers enjoy these luxuries—they were only for a select few.

Attila would place great faith in the words of his shamans, especially when planning battles. The Huns also employed such religious practices as burnt sacrifices and placing horses' skulls in front of their homes to ward off evil.

The religion practiced during Attila's reign proved similar to that of earlier times among the Huns. Some of the features of the Huns' religion involved offering their horses as burnt offerings to their deities. The horses' skulls were also placed in front of their homes to ward off evil. Lacerating their faces as a sign of mourning was another religious practice. In addition, the Huns buried their dead instead of cremating them, placing in the grave personal objects of value such as swords, or bows. Attila himself placed great faith in signs and the words of his priests and soothsayers. They were most important when he planned his military operations. His beliefs in this regard were similar to those of the Greeks and Romans.

Attila's kingdom flourished in every way. Attila had set everything in place: from his circle of intimate followers who carried out his every command to the subject peoples who supplied his society with food and other products. To a great extent, Attila had improved the living conditions of the Huns. However, for the Huns to live prosperously into the future, they had to continue their military operations of subjugating and plundering people. This time, Attila would look to Gaul.

NEW CONQUEST
IN GAUL

At the height of his power from 445 to 450 A.D., Attila sought a new challenge. Annually, he extorted huge sums of gold from the Eastern Roman Empire, which came from Theodosius II and his provinces. Yet Attila had never troubled the western part of the Empire. One of the reasons the Western Empire had been spared the Huns' ravages was due to the region's leader, Aetius. The former child hostage had stayed on friendly terms with Attila, thus keeping him at bay. But when a noble Roman woman, Honoria, sent Attila a ring and a bag of gold in 450 A.D., Attila jumped at the new opportunity.

The woman, Justa Grata Honoria, lived in Ravenna and was Emperor Valentian's sister. Honoria was highly intelligent, ambitious, and self-determined. Growing up, she didn't mind being the heir apparent's sister. She too had a place in line for the throne. She even had the title of "Augusta" conferred on her. After her brother's marriage, however, her status changed. Within a short time, Valentian's

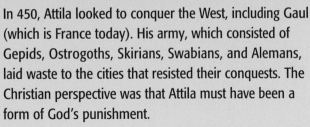

In 450, Attila looked to conquer the West, including Gaul (which is France today). His army, which consisted of Gepids, Ostrogoths, Skirians, Swabians, and Alemans, laid waste to the cities that resisted their conquests. The Christian perspective was that Attila must have been a form of God's punishment.

wife gave birth to a daughter, then another, and Honoria's place in any political or dynastic future disappeared. Neither would she be allowed to marry anyone with ambitions to the throne.

When she turned thirty, Honoria became desperate. She had her own residence within the palace and had a steward who managed it. His name was Eugenius, and in 449 A.D., she had an amorous affair with him. She may have loved him, but that fact was incidental to her plans. The two hatched a plot for Eugenius to murder Valentian. The plot was discovered, and Eugenius was put to death. Honoria's part in the plan resulted in her being discharged from the palace. As if this turn of events wasn't enough for her to deal with, Honoria soon became compulsorily betrothed to a rich senator of good character, Flavius Bossus Herculanus. He had assured the emperor that his wife-to-be would not be able to draw him into any revolutionary schemes.

Honoria was more distressed than ever over her coming marriage to this man whom she did not want to marry. She pondered over what to do, and in a flash, she decided to turn for help from a barbarian power. So, she sent a trustworthy servant, a eunuch named Hyacinthus, with her ring and some gold to Attila, asking his help. She hoped he would come to her aid and prevent this distasteful marriage. She also thought that Attila, the most powerful monarch in Europe, would champion her cause.

However, Attila interpreted her message to be a marriage proposal. Thus, Attila claimed her as his bride, and also wanted half of Valentian's territory as her dowry. He also determined then and there to invade the western provinces and made his plans accordingly. In a clever move, Attila then sent a letter—not to Valentian in Ravenna, but to Theodosius in Constantinople—demanding Honoria as his bride. Theodosius quickly advised Valentian to hand Honoria over to Attila. When Valentian discovered what Honoria had done, Hyacinthus was tortured and beheaded. Valentian's mother intervened with him to spare Honoria's life.

When Attila found out about Honoria's treatment, he sent an ambassador to Ravenna in protest. He insisted the lady had done no wrong, and that she had simply wished to marry him, and he would come to the court enforcing her right to a share in the Empire. Of course, Attila had looked longingly toward the Atlantic for some time, hoping to include Gaul in his extended kingdom.

As Attila mustered his forces, Valentian had to decide

quickly what to do. His mother (and regent), Placida, had died in 450, and the emperor Theodosius had also died that same year. So Valentian had neither of his trusted counselors to help him. He was forced to make his own decisions in the looming crisis with Attila.

In the meantime, Attila and a huge army—made up of Gepids, Ostroboths, Skirians, Swabians, and Alemans—were already on their way to Gaul. The most likely route that Attila followed would have been a road the Romans had built from the outskirts of modern-day Budapest to modern-day Vienna. From there, they would have followed along the Danube, through an area that now contains vineyards and castles.

From this area, Attila's army entered the Rhineland territory so he could join up with the Franks, with whom he had an alliance. The army also crossed the Rhine River at some point, then followed along the Moselle River. They also took possession of Trier, an important city on the Moselle. The city had been the residence of emperors, had been fortified by Augustus, and was known as Roma Secunda.

The city of Metz lay further up on the Moselle and was a strategic military and ecclesiastical center. Julius Caesar had described the city as one of the oldest and most important in Gaul, and it was not an easy city to capture. The siege of Metz began on April 7, 451. Gregory of Tours, a fifth-century religious leader, wrote of the Huns' attack, "The Huns, issuing from Pannonia, reached the town of Metz on the vigil of the feast of Easter, devastating the whole country. They gave the city to the flames and slew the people with the edge of the sword, and did to death the priests of the Lord before the holy altars." One building was spared: the oratory of the deacon Stephen. Gregory noted that "The blessed deacon Stephen, conferring with the holy apostles Peter and Paul about this destruction, said: 'I beseech you suffer not the city of Metz to be burned to the ground by the enemy.'"

Stephen thought the wicked deeds of the city might be so

Although Attila's destruction of cities was very thorough, there would be a few times when displays of Christian devotion would move Attila to the point where he would spare a city the wrath of his army. In Paris, a girl named Genevieve confronted Attila with a group of virgins and successfully saved it from harm. Genevieve is now celebrated as the patron saint of Paris.

great that God allowed its destruction. He asked, however, that his oratory might be spared. The apostles assured him to "Go in peace, most beloved brother, this oratory of thine alone shall be spared in the fire. For the city we shall not obtain this grace, seeing that the sentence of divine judgment is already gone forth upon it. The sin of the people is grown so great, and the sound of their wickedness is gone up before the Lord. For this cause shall this city be burned with fire."

The Christian chroniclers attributed any city being destroyed to the city's sins—but if it was spared, it was thanks to divine intervention and the lives of the pious. None of them gave Attila and his army credit for superior military skills. They thought of him merely as God's instrument of punishment, or the "Scourge of God," as they called him. As Attila's army made its way through Gaul, certain cities offered resistance. Most of these places were not only larger and fortified cities, but their bishops also played a part in their ability to resist.

One of the important cities on Attila's route was Rheims, where a bishopric had been set up in the third century. In the fifth century, Clovis, king of the Franks, was baptized by St. Remiguius, and the oil used in the ceremony was said to have been brought from heaven by a dove. The city may have been on Attila's route. His army followed along riverbeds as opposed to taking the Roman roads.

Another less important city that Attila planned to visit was Lutetia, or Paris. For many centuries, Lutetia was only a fortified island on the Seine. The emperor Julian, for one, however, loved the quaint city. Emperor Julian wrote of Lutetia: "I happened to be in winter quarters at my beloved Lutetia—for that is how the Celts call the capital of the Parisians. It is a small island lying in the river. A wall entirely surrounds it, and wooden bridges lead to it on both sides. The river seldom rises and falls, but usually is the same depth in the winter as in the summer season, and it provides water which is very clear to the eye and very pleasant for one who wishes to drink. As the inhabitants live on an island they have to draw their water chiefly from the river."

Although Attila had his sights set on Paris, a girl by the name of Genevieve had dedicated herself to a life of faith. In one of the city's churches, Genevieve offered to go alone to confront Attila, or with a group of virgins. She prophesied that Paris would be spared an attack by Attila, and she proved correct. She became the patron saint of Paris, and her spirit has been invoked at different times in the city's history.

Another person who intervened for the city of Troyes was Bishop St. Loup. Gregory of Tours wrote, "In 451 the savage Attila, King of his Huns, who had already destroyed Reims, Langres, Besancon and several other cities, marched on Troyes. The whole town was in a state of fear. The Bishop, St. Loup, decided to save his people. After praying and fasting he donned his pontifical garb and, full of confidence in God, left the town to meet the barbarians." When he met the king of the Huns, the bishop asked him, "Who are you?" Attila replied, "I am the Scourge of God." The bishop said to Attila, "If indeed you are the Scourge of God, do only that which God allows you." The bishop's words and his saintliness moved Attila, and he spared the city of Troyes.

By the time Attila reached Orleans, he encountered unexpected resistance. Two armies—the Roman army headed by Aetius, and the Visigoth army led by King Theodoric and his son Thorismond—had arrived at the beleaguered city to defend it. Attila was about to be challenged as never before.

For Attila to encounter resistance was a new and upsetting experience for him. In his other campaigns in the Balkans, Germany, and even in France, he had expected cities to surrender to him—otherwise, he would destroy them as he wished. Attila had also had secret plans to be joined by Sangiban, king of the Alans, who had promised to deliver both Arles and Orleans to Attila. But Aetius learned of the plot and foiled it.

Aetius, on the other hand, needed to have the support of the Visgoths and their leader, Theodoric. He was not certain until nearly the time of battle that they would fight on the Roman side. Aetius found another ally in Avitus, a retired Roman senator, who agreed to be an intermediary between Aetius and Theodoric. When Avitus spoke to Theodoric, he prophesied the terrible destruction if the Huns won the battle. He appealed to the Visigoths as Christians, and Theodoric was finally persuaded to side with Aetius. Other groups then joined Aetius' army: the Alans, Burgundians, Franks, Saxons, and, of course, the Visigoths.

When Attila realized he was about to engage in a major battle, he called for his shamanite priests to foretell the outcome. As they examined the cattle entrails and streaks from scraped bones, they came to a disturbing conclusion: the Huns would be defeated in battle! They made another prophecy as well—that the commander of the opposing forces would be killed in battle. Attila interpreted this to mean that Aetius would be the one who would die.

Attila chose the battle site. He realized now that his earlier tactics wouldn't work this time. But he knew he needed an open terrain to give his cavalry the best benefit. So, he advanced northward and crossed the Seine River. Aetius' army followed.

The site of the battle was near the city of Chalons. According to Jordanes, Attila addressed his troops before the battle began, saying, "Here you stand after conquering mighty nations and subduing the world. I therefore think it foolish for me to goad you with words, as though you were men who had not been proved in action. Let a new leader or an untried army resort to that. It is not right for me to say anything common, nor ought you to listen. For what is war but your usual custom?" After pausing to catch a breath, Attila continued: "Or what is sweeter for a brave man than to seek revenge with his own hand? It is a right of nature to glut the soul with vengeance. Let us then attack the foe eagerly, for they are ever bolder who make the attack." The Battle of Chalons was fought in late June of 451, and has been described as one of the 15 decisive battles of the world.

The battle was one that engaged unusually large forces—and the nations involved ranged from the Volga to the Atlantic. A sixth-century Ostrogoth scholar and administrator, Cassiodorus, described the battle as "A conflict fierce, various, obstinate and bloody, such as could not be paralleled either in the present or in past ages."

The battle commenced toward sunset as soldiers on horseback rode from each side to gain a ridge above the plain. Roman horse archers wearing mail and scale armor rushed forward and were joined by Visigoth nobles and their retainers, who wielded lances and swords, and the group captured one side. The Huns charged down the other slope with their allied

When it seemed as if Attila's army would be defeated by Aetius, Attila prepared a large funeral pyre for himself, as he was determined not to be taken alive by the enemy. Fortunately, Aetius persuaded the Visigoths to go home and allowed the Huns to escape.

German tribes. A great struggle began for the crest of the hill. Archers shot arrows from a distance while Germanic warriors fought hand-to-hand with each other. A squadron of Alans faced the Huns, their former masters. Aetius doubted their loyalty, so he placed them between the Romans on the left wing and the Visigoths on the right so they could not easily escape. Attila sent the bravest and finest warriors in the center with the Ostrogoths and other subject Germans on either side. The fight for the hill continued and foot soldiers entered the fray. The

Franks allied with the Romans threw their famed tomahawk axes at the enemy before dashing into close combat.

The Romans and the Visigoths finally gained the upper hand and pursued the Huns back down the hill. Attila tried to rally his men with words of encouragement. Theodoric also rallied his Visigoth troops as they fought against their close kinsmen, the Ostrogoths. Both sides fought with a vengeance, and in the thick of the battle, Theodoric was struck dead. The Visigoths, angered by Theodoric's death, chased the Huns back, falling upon many of them and causing the Huns and their allies to flee. Attila and the body of his army took a hasty retreat behind the wagons of their encampment. As the day came to a close, the exhausted warriors sought refuge in their own camps.

The following day, an observer noted that "Each side awoke to the awful spectacle of a battlefield heaped with the slain and wounded. Slashed and cut warriors stumbled back to their tribal groups. If bound cleanly, their lacerations would heal. Those pierced by lance and arrow, bursting vital organs, stood little chance. Arrows with barbed heads ripped great holes in their skin. Those fired by the Huns were believed to be tipped with poison . . . Inflammation and putrefaction set in and warriors groaned as sickness and disease claimed many still left alive after the shock of combat."

The Visigoths, seemingly undismayed by the carnage, wanted to finish the battle with the Huns and wreak vengeance for their fallen leader. Attila had piled saddles within his wagons to form a fire upon which he would throw himself, for he was determined not to be taken alive. But Aetius persuaded the Visigoths to go home—in particular, Theodoric's son, so he could claim his throne. By so doing, Aetius allowed the Huns to retreat, perhaps as a final favor for the Huns. However, Aetius' judgment was flawed, for Attila and the Huns would not simply fade away—they would most certainly seek revenge for their awesome defeat.

INVASION
OF ITALY

Defeat in battle and Aetius' decision to let the Huns retreat left Attila baffled. He remained immobilized at first on the battle-field to see if the enemy would try some new strategy. When nothing happened, he began to withdraw.

Bishop St. Loup guided Attila as far as the Rhine, although he may have been taken as a prisoner. The Huns committed more atrocities on their return home. According to Edward Gibbon, "They massacred their hostages as well as their captives; two hundred young maidens were tortured with exquisite and unrelenting rage; their bodies torn asunder by wild horses, or their bones were crushed under the weight of rolling waggons; and their unburied limbs were abandoned on the public roads as a prey to dogs."

As soon as Attila reached Hungary, he again made demands for large quantities of gold from Constantinople, since spoils from the recent war had not materialized. He demanded the gold that made

After the Gaul campaign, Attila set his sights on Rome after Emperor Marcian refused to continue paying tribute to the Huns. This depiction shows Attila invading Rome with angels and other heavenly (and Christian) figures watching from above.

up his annual tribute from the Eastern Empire. However, since Theodosius' death, his son-in-law, Marcian, had become the new emperor. He had decided not to give the Huns any more gold, although neither did he want to engage them in any military action at this time.

Marcian did send an embassy under the command of Apollonius, but when Attila learned that he would no longer receive tribute, he refused to let him cross the Danube. He also threatened the Eastern Empire with war, but then decided against the move. However, he planned a new strategy, one he must have been considering for some time: he decided to invade Italy.

To Attila, invading Italy was the consequence of demanding half the Western Empire as Honoria's dowry. If Attila had captured Rome, he would have followed in Alaric's footsteps forty years earlier. But since Attila failed to achieve his goal in Gaul and was doubting his capacity (with diminished manpower) to succeed in the Balkans, the logical next step would be Italy. He and the Huns needed to plunder for their economy to survive. He also may have learned that Aetius had only retained a small number of the huge force in Gaul.

Thus, Attila and his troops set out for northern Italy in the spring of 452. He was again at the helm of an international force, including many Germanic peoples. Attila followed a route through the Klagenfurt gap, and one that paralleled the present border between Italy and Slovenia. On his route to Italy, Alaric had followed much the same route.

Moving toward Trieste, the army stopped at Aquileia, a city with much history. In the past, Aquileia was a fortified city of some importance, but today it is only a small village. Located inland, and at the head of the Adriatic Sea, Aquileia was founded by the Romans. The Romans founded the city intending to halt barbaric invaders from entering Italy after crossing the Julian Alps. In time, the city became a strategic commercial center as well as a military post.

Ausonius called it the fourth greatest city in Italy after Rome, Milan, and Capua, and in 10 B.C., Augustus, who had taken up residence there, received Herod the Great. The city also became the capital of Venetia, and enjoyed the prestige at one time of being the second city in Italy that could mint coins. In addition, whoever captured Aquileia could control much of northern Italy.

The Romans considered Aquileia impregnable — that is, before Attila arrived with his forces. Alaric, earlier, had bypassed the city. But Attila decided to lay siege to the city. Yet month after month, the city of Aquileia resisted Attila's siege.

Concern over the city ate away at Attila. Every week that passed, army supplies got lower and lower, and their dependency for forage on the local countryside increased. At the end of three months, Attila thought about giving up. In fact, Attila had given orders to his army to be prepared to leave at sunrise the following day. Then, he beheld a "sign" that he was not to leave. Procopius wrote: "The following day about sunrise the barbarians had raised the siege and were already beginning their departure when a single male stork, which had a nest on a certain tower of the city wall and was rearing its nestlings there, suddenly rose and left the place with his young. The father stork was flying, but the little storks, since they were not yet quite ready to fly, were at times sharing their father's flight and at times riding on his back, and thus they flew off and went away from the city." Attila's observation of the stork led him to believe he was to continue the siege. A short time later, the very place on the wall where the stork had nested cracked, fell down, and Attila and his men entered the city.

Attila's army totally devastated the city of Aquileia — in fact, it never recovered from the destruction to become the important city it had been. The destruction of Aquileia early in Attila's campaign greatly encouraged him. The next city of Metz fared about the same as Aquileia. News of Attila's conquests spread throughout Italy as people in various cities did what they could to prepare for his onslaught. From Aquileia, Attila's army followed along the Po River with all intentions

A group of Huns pillaging a villa in Italy on their campaign. Soon, whole cities would flee upon hearing of Attila's advance.

of continuing on to Rome. He headed south toward Milan—an unconventional route, but one that was less likely to allow for an encounter with an enemy army.

Aetius, in the meantime, did not have a large army at his command. He no longer had the Alans or the Visigoths, and since the Roman army was made up largely of foreign peoples, the Romans were now unable to resist their foe.

The next city Attila encountered was Padua, another

important city with a flourishing economy based on agriculture and industry. Like Aquileia, Padua suffered great losses under the Huns. Many of Padua's citizens fled before the approaching army. These 500 people later founded the city of Venice. The Roman historian Cassiodorus reported that "Many families of Aquileia, Padua, and the adjacent towns . . . found a safe, though obscure, refuge in the neighbouring islands [near present-day Venice]. . . . Till the middle of the fifth century these remote and sequestered spots remained without cultivation, with few inhabitants. . . . But the manners of the Venetian fugitives, their arts and their government, were gradually formed by their new situation."

Attila soon attained the cities of Vicenza and Verona. Of the two, Verona contained many magnificent buildings like the amphitheatre, which was built in the first century. The city also collected the inheritance taxes for all of northern Italy—making it quite possible that Attila gained much plunder from the conquest of Verona. Other cities along Attila's route included Brescia, Bergamo, and Milan.

Attila knew the ways of the Romans well, and no doubt calculated that Aetius would not be able to raise much of an army. Nevertheless, Aetius wanted to have a face-off with Attila and his troops. But Emperor Valentian III was not in favor of it. He chose, instead, to leave Ravenna for Rome. Valentian, a dedicated Christian, had few options for his tottering empire. It is most likely he left Ravenna for Rome in the hope of finding some way to resist Attila.

In the meantime, Attila continued his march down the Italian peninsula and reached the old city of Milano, the fourth-century capital of the Western Roman Empire. The emperor Constantine had issued his famous edict here, officially recognizing the Christian religion. Again, in Milano, Attila encountered no resistance. For a brief time, Attila took over the palace. In the palace, his attention was drawn to a picture of the Caesars sitting on thrones with Scythian princes at their feet. The artist was brought to Attila and ordered to change the image so that the Roman emperors would be shown kneeling before the throne of Attila and emptying bags of gold in tribute.

After leaving Milano, Attila's army marched toward Pavia, then known as Ticinum. From there, the army advanced haphazardly, seemingly without any destination. Attila and his forces soon ended up near Mantua, where Pope Leo I himself faced him.

Leo had had the title of "Great" conferred on him by the Catholic Church. In addition, Leo I had begun as pope in 440 and continued for twenty-one years. During his time in office, he witnessed the decline of the Western Roman Empire while the Church in the West had risen to power. Much of the Church's growing power was due to Leo's personality, faith, and administrative skills.

The pope held the Empire in great esteem. He recognized its importance spiritually and materially. He also recognized the responsibility placed on the Roman Empire to spread Christianity, and as he himself said: "That the consequences of this unspeakable generosity might be made known throughout the whole world divine providence fashioned the Roman Empire, the growth of which was extended to boundaries so wide that all races everywhere became next-door neighbours."

Further, the pope was always aware of his succession to St. Peter—and as such, his great responsibilities. Even when Leo spoke or wrote a letter, he sensed the guidance of St. Peter. He also took upon himself the responsibility of improving the priesthood. He was especially concerned about priests practicing *usury* (collecting interest on loans). Because of his convictions, he banned the ordination of those required to participate in any kind of hereditary labor. The man of God must be free, he believed, from other obligations.

Pope Leo I, or Leo the Great, went out to confront Attila and persuaded Attila to not attack Rome. It may have been that Leo's words were persuasive, but there are also accounts that claim Attila saw a vision of St. Peter and St. Paul, threatening death if Attila did not do as Leo asked. The two saints can clearly be seen in this painting above Leo.

Believing in absolute authority, the pope did not condone dissent. Valentian had even issued a pronouncement calling upon Gaul's bishops to submit to Leo. The pope also made it understood that he would not allow the heresy of Manichaeism within the Church. Manichaeism combines

Christian and pagan elements, and sees a continuing struggle between the kingdom of light and the kingdom of darkness. Pope Leo made other pronouncements such as those on the sanctity of Christian marriage, but he was not an outstanding theologian—the realm of profound theology remained in the hands of the Eastern Church. There, scholars had the benefit of the Christian gospel, Greek philosophy, and Eastern mysticism. Leo's strengths were in his clear, level-headed judgments, and in his abilities as an administrator as well as an inspiring preacher.

Because of the respect he enjoyed from his contemporaries, Pope Leo was called on by them to confront Attila face to face. The meeting took place in the summer of 452 on the banks of the Mincio River. The pope did not go alone. Two other men went with him: Trigetius, the Prefect of Rome and an experienced negotiator who had come to terms with the Vandal king Geiseric in Africa fifteen years earlier; and Gennadius Avienus, a rich and powerful politician who held a post involving Rome's water supplies. The men came to ask Attila not to attack Rome.

When the men reached Attila, he was resting in his tent. He continued to recline while the three men used all their powers of persuasion on him. Pope Leo impressed Attila most of all, not only by his eloquence, according to later chroniclers, but "by his pontifical robes and by his majestic aspect. The climax came when St. Peter and St. Paul appeared alongside the Pope and threatened Attila with instant death unless he acceded to the Pope's request." Whether Attila acquiesced to Pope Leo and the other men because of divine intervention or not, he could have received the pope's visit as a "sign" similar to others he had received in Aquileia, and earlier, before the Battle of Chalons. As a result of the meeting, Attila and his men turned back, and Rome was spared.

Attila also needed to reach Hungary before winter came. Undoubtedly, the Hun army had gained much in plunder from their time in Italy, so Attila was well pleased with his campaign. Now, he was anxious to get home and enjoy the rewards of his Italian invasion. But as Attila was first and foremost a warrior, he had to plan new conquests to be satisfied. He would return home and decide what to do next.

9

FINAL DAYS

The new emperor in Constantinople, Marcian, proved to be somewhat of a concern to Attila. Attila stepped up his program of sending ambassadors and threatening letters to Marcian. In effect, he warned him to continue the gold payments or he would destroy his empire. Since the emperor seemed in no hurry to comply with Attila's wishes, Attila was most likely planning a maneuver against Marcian.

Indeed, Attila did launch an offensive in the winter of 452-453, but it involved fighting the Alans. By reducing the Alans, Attila hoped to become a menace to the Visigoths. He left Dacia and Pannonia planning to cross the Loire River where the Alans lived. But according to the chronicler Jordanes, as Attila lead his army against the Alans, "Thorismond, King of the Visigoths, with the quickness of thought, perceived Attila's trick. By forced marches he came to the Alani before him and was well prepared to check the advance of

After enjoying a wedding celebration, Attila was found dead the next morning with his young and terrified bride, thinking she would be accused of killing him. After a life of warfare and hardship, it seemed that a burst artery ultimately felled the king of the Huns.

Attila when he came after him. They joined battle in almost the same way as before at the Catalaunian Plains, and Thorismund dashed his hopes of victory, for he routed him and drove him from the land without a triumph, compelling him to flee to his own country."

By the spring of 453, Attila was enjoying his life back in

Hungary, and to celebrate his considerable successes, he decided to take a new wife. The young and beautiful Ildico would become Attila's new bride. The wedding turned out to be cause for a huge celebration in Attila's wooden palace on the banks of the Tisza River. Drinking and merrymaking went on throughout the evening, and Attila retired late. Late the following morning, Attila's attendants wondered why he had not appeared, and suspecting foul play, they broke the door down. As Jordanes wrote: "There they found the death of Attila accomplished by an effusion of blood, without any wound, and the girl with downcast face weeping beneath her veil." The report said that Attila had burst an artery, and that he had suffocated on his own blood. The poor Ildico obviously feared for her life, no doubt thinking she would be accused of causing Attila's demise.

The Huns laid Attila's body under a silk pavilion in the center of the plain. Then, the most skillful horsemen proceeded to gallop wildly around the body to gladden the heart of their fallen leader. They sang a hymn that told of the greatness of Attila. The lyrics told how he was the greatest of all the Hun kings, son of Mundzuk, lord of the most heroic of peoples, who ruled with might over Scythian and Germanic lands, and also filled the Roman Empire with fear, took their cities, and exacted tribute from them.

According to custom, Attila's male followers cut off much of their hair and slashed their faces so their leader could be mourned by the blood of warriors, not by the cries of women. Then, as Jordanes says: "In the secrecy of night, they buried his body in the earth. They bound his coffins, the first with gold, the second with silver, and the third with the strength of iron. They also added the arms of foemen won in the fight, trappings of rare worth, sparkling with gems, and ornaments of all sorts whereby princely state is maintained." To ensure that the "great riches" buried with Attila might not tempt the grave diggers, they were killed after digging Attila's grave.

Speculation arose soon after Attila's death that he was

poisoned by his bride, although no proof exists. In addition, the burial site for the body has never been located. An archeologist believes Attila's body was placed in a coffin with rare treasures and buried in the earth and may still be found one day. But even if it is found, the body would be hard to identify because there are no words of inscription. The burial site is somewhere between the Tisza and Danube Rivers—an area that measures around twenty thousand square kilometers. Only the site of Alexander the Great's burial place has raised as much speculation as Attila's.

Attila's kingship over the Huns lasted a short eight years. Yet, during that time, he had an enormous impact on his contemporaries. Much of this impact came from his many conquests. In an eight-year period, for him to have held both the Eastern and Western Roman Empires at bay and exacted ransoms from them seems incredible. He constantly threatened them with destruction if they refused to comply with his wishes. He also overran much of Germany and France.

Objectively speaking, his achievements were not all that unique. Others had gone before him and surpassed him, and even won victories that endured. Alaric had conquered Rome while Attila did not. Athaulf the Visigoth took territory in France, and Geiseric the Vandal took areas of North Africa, which his people inhabited for centuries. Attila added no territory to the kingdom of his forefathers.

Yet, Attila was both feared and respected more than any of the other military leaders of his day or of the decades preceding him. His race and religion can explain some of his mystique. The other leaders, the Visigoths, Ostrogoths, Vandals, Franks, and others were mainly Christians, and with more liberal policies adopted by the Romans, could become Roman citizens. They may not have been appreciated by well-born Romans but were thought capable of achieving success as Roman citizens.

Attila was an outsider: he was neither a Christian nor a Roman citizen. Further, his followers were thought of as alien,

To many, Attila was, as shown in this picture, a barbaric invader who laid waste to all that was holy. To others, especially those who came in direct contact with him, he was seen as a modest man with dignity and compassion.

crude, and frightening. That he was able to command so many men of different races under him who appeared to be loyal to him was an impressive feat. Many of these men, especially those in his inner circle, chose to come with him and be part of his regime. Further, there is little if any evidence that his supporters deserted him. Aetius, on the other hand, who was an acknowledged leader of men with the might of the Roman Empire behind him, had a continual problem with army deserters. Attila had on his side his compelling personality, leadership ability, and reputation.

Attila's personality and conquests have often seemed paradoxical to his contemporaries. The Roman Priscus, who knew Attila personally, provides the sole account of what he was like. Priscus claimed that he was "a man of dignity and compassion, modest in his personal habits and requirements, holding a court that attracted thoughtful men of a variety of nations." Conversely, St. Jerome, a sophisticated, and well-educated Church Father, wrote about the Huns as though they were cannibals, and thought their way of life was completely despicable.

Was Attila an outstanding ruler and a great military commander? The writer Jordanes thought so. He reported: "Attila was lord over all the Huns and almost the sole earthly ruler of all the tribes of Scythia, a man marvellous for his glorious fame among all nations." Some modern Hungarian authorities maintain that Attila's immediate predecessors, rather than Attila, raised the Hun kingdom to the level that it could take on the Roman Empire and have that Empire fear and respect it. One of these same authorities admitted, however, that if Attila had lived longer, he could have successfully attacked the Western Empire, and history would have been changed.

Any verdicts on Attila's achievements need to be based on what his aims were. If he wanted to enlarge the Hun kingdom, he clearly failed. If he planned to conquer much of the known world, his time was cut short. However, if his main achievements were the consolidation of the Hun kingdom and enrichment of its economy by his marauding warriors, he found success, and proved to be his nation's benefactor.

ATTILA'S
LEGACY

After Attila's death and the ascension of his eldest son Ellak to the throne, there was a shift back to the old system. Although Ellak had the continuing support of Onegesius, Attila's main administrator, two of his brothers had other ideas. The two younger sons, Dengizik and Ernak, wanted to have a share in ruling the Huns, similar to the arrangement when Bleda and Attila were co-rulers.

Although Ellak complied with their wishes, the result was a return to the old nomadic way of individual tribesmen each ruling their tribes. The reversal also brought problems. Not much thought was given to the new strength the subordinate people under Attila had acquired and had come to expect, especially when fighting under Attila's command. The new division also guaranteed instability in the kingdom. Fighting broke out between the brothers' factions within a year of Attila's death. Ellak was able to settle the dispute, while the younger brothers fled the territory. But now, Ellak faced a more

While Attila's achievements were tremendous, things began to fall apart after his death. In the hands of his sons, the Huns experienced diplomatic and military defeats and were soon begging the Romans for land instead of dictating terms of tribute.

serious problem: Ardaric, King of the Gepids, and Attila's most reliable ally, had rebelled against Hun rule. In this he had the support of Emperor Marcian of Constantinople.

In 454, near the River Nedao in Pannonia, the Huns fought

a battle against a combined force of Gepids and a variety of Germanic and Iranian peoples. The outcome of the battle proved more decisive than that of the Catalaunian Fields near Chalon in determining the fate of the Hun people. Ardaric's army won an overwhelming victory, and Ellak was killed. The defeat of the Huns was one from which they would never recover.

The Gepids, whom the Huns had regarded as the peasant farmers who supplied them with food, were the immediate recipients of the Hun Empire, the part of Hungary that stretched between the Danube and the Tisza. Emperor Marcian also benefited from the battle's outcome. He consolidated his power, and territory was rearranged according to his wishes. His empire could finally enjoy freedom from the Huns' attacks. The Ostrogoths and Marcian also agreed on a formal treaty in which he assigned them land in northern Pannonia.

Meanwhile, Attila's sons Dengizik and Ernak, along with their Hun followers, were forced to settle in the lower reaches of the Danube. They wanted to be established permanently there and sent an embassy in 466 to Emperor Leo I, who had succeeded Marcian. The Huns also wanted to have a free market on the Danube like they had had in the past. But the emperor refused their request, as he was not interested in the Huns' concerns. The Huns returned home in failure.

Attila's son Dengizik acted in true Hun fashion to the emperor's refusal. He mustered his troops in 466-467 and led them across the frozen Danube. He sent another embassy to Emperor Leo stating his terms—to pay up or else. The emperor refused his request and demanded obedience to imperial rule. The result was war, and in the fighting that followed, Dengizik's forces withstood those of Anthemius for two years. But in 469, Anagestes became general and conquered the Huns in a total defeat. Wildly celebrated in Constantinople, the victory provided rejoicing for years to come, and Dengizik's skull was placed on prominent display.

A typical scene from a Hun conquest, and one of Attila's enduring legacies—that of the merciless conqueror from the East who spread fear and destruction wherever he went. Unfortunately, his sons could not capitalize upon their father's reputation, and the Huns' power was greatly reduced.

Attila's son Ernak proved the more careful of the two brothers. When he realized that the odds against him in the combined forces of the Bulgars and the Romans, he begged Leo for land, and for his people to have a part in the Empire. Leo granted his requests, and the Huns remained in the Dobruja

This scene shows Attila—who was also known as "Etzel" in German—entering the city of Vienna. His reputation and legend still live on today—Giuseppe Verdi wrote an opera entitled *Attila,* and a recent book entitled *Leadership Secrets of Attila the Hun* attempted to use examples of Attila's leadership and apply them to modern management.

area betwen the Danube and the Black Sea in present-day Romania. The difference between Attila's exploits and achievements and those of his sons could hardly have been greater.

When Attila first emerged on the world scene, Christian preachers—in this instance, Ephraim the Syrian—compared him (and the Huns) to the Antichrist spoken of in the Bible. In the book of Ezekiel in the Old Testament, the prophet warns: "And lo, son of man, say in prophecy to Gog: 'The Lord Yahweh says this: Is it not true that you are planning to set out at a time when Israel is living undisturbed? You plan to leave your home in the far north, you and many nations with you, a great army of countless troops all mounted. You plan to invade Israel my people."

Shortly after Attila's death, legends began to form about him. Undoubtedly, some of the legends go back to the unusual—and frightening—appearance of the Huns to Europeans. Their slashed faces, often from burial rites, and strange, mongoloid features were terrifying—and the horses they rode were frightening as well.

Another aspect of the Huns' reputation rested on the food they ate. Ammianus explained: "They are so hardy that they neither require fire nor well-flavoured food, but live on the roots of such herbs as they get in the fields, or on the half-raw flesh of any animal, which they merely warm rapidly by placing it between their own thighs and the back of their horses."

St. Jerome pointed out yet another facet of the Huns' (and Attila's) reputation: "Speeding hither and thither on their nimble-footed horses, they were filling all the world with panic and bloodshed. They outstripped rumour in speed, and, when they came, they spared neither religion nor rank nor age, even for wailing children they had no pity. . . . it was generally agreed that the goal of the invaders was Jerusalem."

Destiny prepared Attila well for the role he was to play. Coming from a barbaric background to the Roman court at Ravenna, Attila brought with him a keen, native intelligence. Following his time at the court, he traveled among the Hun people and practiced his persuasive abilities on them. He urged them to come together as one and to put aside tribal rivalries.

By the time Attila became the king of the Huns, he was able to lead his people with a commanding presence. He possessed all the important leadership qualities, including the ability to act quickly and decisively. He also surrounded himself with people who could supply those abilities he lacked. His inner circle formed a cohesive group, and Attila rewarded his loyal followers with praise as well as gifts—another important quality for a leader.

An artist's depiction of Attila the Hun following his defeat at Chalons, in one of the rare illustrations that do not show him at one of his more victorious moments. However, the Battle of Chalons is considered to be one of the 15 most decisive battles of the world.

Legends of Attila appear in many languages and among many peoples. Artists have depicted him in paintings, sculpture, and even on coins. Tales have been told about him, usually portraying him as some type of animal or as a demon. In a church in Uppland, Sweden, Attila appears in a fresco as a dog-headed archer. The composer Giuseppe Verdi wrote an opera simply titled *Attila*.

Artistic depictions and narratives continue to be written about Attila. Nearly every schoolchild knows about Attila the Hun. His commanding presence and charismatic personality have come down through the centuries in an enduring "larger than life" persona. Attila, the king of the Huns, came from outside Western civilization and took on the Roman Empire itself, often bringing it to its knees. He stood out as one man against many—and won, at least for a time. To the Christian church, he was, as he himself said, "the Scourge of God." He remains one of history's most fascinating figures.

406 A.D. Attila the Hun born near Tisza River on Hungarian Plain. The Hun chief Uldin forms alliance with the Roman general Stilicho.

408 Uldin penetrates deep into Thrace and Illyricum; many of his troops defect to the Roman Army.

410 Huns stage seagoing raids around the Black Sea.

417 King Mundzuk dies; Rugila becomes king. Attila goes as child hostage to Ravenna to live in the court of Honorius.

422 Attila leaves Honorius' court; travels to the Hun tribes.

433 Rugila dies. Attila and Bleda become co-rulers.

434 Treaty of Margus is signed between the Romans and the Huns.

441–443 The Huns raid Illyricum and the Western Balkan provinces.

445 Huns fight the Akatziri; Bleda dies.

447 Huns attack Thrace again and approach Constantinople.

449 Attila undertakes diplomatic mission to the East Roman Empire.

451 Attila and Huns invade Gaul; sustain heavy losses at Battle of Chalons.

452 Huns invade Italy, capturing and looting Aquileia, Milan, and other cities; Pope Leo I intervenes and they turn back from Rome.

453 Attila dies.

Adkins, Lesley and Roy. *Introduction to the Romans*. London: Quantum Books Publishing, 1991.

Baum, Franz H., and Birnbaum, Marianna, eds. *Attila: The Man and His Image*. Budapest: Corvina, 1993.

Howarth, Patrick. *Attila, King of the Huns*. London: Constable Books, 1994.

Maenchen-Helfen, Otto J. *The World of the Huns*. Los Angeles: University of California Press, 1973.

Malcolm, Todd. *The Barbarians*. New York: G.P. Putnam's Sons, 1972.

Newark, Tim. *The Barbarians*. New York: Sterling Publishing Company, 1988.

Roberts, Wess. *Victory Secrets of Attila the Hun*. New York: Doubleday, 1993.

Thompson, E.A. *The Huns*. Cambridge, Mass.: Blackwell Publishers, LTD, 1996.

Adkins, Lesley and Roy. *Introduction to the Romans*. London: Quantum Books Publishing, 1991.

Baum, Franz H., and Birnbaum, Marianna, eds. *Attila: The Man and His Image*. Budapest: Corvina, 1993.

Gordon, C. D. *The Age of Attila*. Ann Arbor: University of Michigan Press, 1973.

Howarth, Patrick. *Attila, King of the Huns*. London: Constable Books, 1994.

Maenchen-Helfen, Otto J. *The World of the Huns*. Los Angeles: University of California Press, 1973.

Nardo, Don. *The Fall of the Roman Empire*. San Diego: Greenhaven Press, 1988.

Roberts, Wess. *Victory Secrets of Attila the Hun*. New York: Doubleday, 1993.

Thompson, E. A. *The Huns*. Cambridge, MA: Blackwell Publishers, 1996.

Todd, Malcolm. *The Barbarians*. London: Batsford, 1972.

Vardy, Steven Bela. *Attila*. New York: Chelsea House Publications, 1991.

page:

11: Hierophant Collection
13: Hierophant Collection
17: © Chris Hellier/Corbis
20: © Bettmann/Corbis
23: Hierophant Collection
26: Hulton Archive/Getty Images
29: © Bettmann/Corbis
32: Hierophant Collection
34: Hierophant Collection
37: Hierophant Collection
40: Hierophant Collection
46: © Bettmann/Corbis
49: © Hulton-Deutsch Collection/Corbis
53: Hierophant Collection

56: Hierophant Collection
59: © Hulton Archive/Getty Images
62: Erich Lessing/Art Resource, NY
66: Hierophant Collection
69: © Hulton Archive/Getty Images
72: © Bettmann/Corbis
75: © Archivo iconografico, S.A./Corbis
79: © Bettmann/Corbis
82: © Bettmann/Corbis
85: Alinari/Art Resource, NY
87: Hierophant Collection
88: Erich Lessing/Art Resource, NY
90: Hierophant Collection

Cover: © Bettmann/Corbis

Frontis: Hierophant Collection

BONNIE CARMAN HARVEY is a freelance writer, teacher, and public speaker who holds a doctorate in English. She has written numerous biographies, conducts writing workshops, and is a former movie review editor and film critic. Among her historical biographies are *Jane Addams: Nobel Prize Winner and Founder of Hull House* and *Daniel Webster: Liberty and Union, Now and Forever.*

ARTHUR M. SCHLESINGER, JR. is the leading American historian of our time. He won the Pulitzer Prize for his book *The Age of Jackson* (1945) and again for a chronicle of the Kennedy Administration, *A Thousand Days* (1965), which also won the National Book Award. Professor Schlesinger is the Albert Schweitzer Professor of the Humanities at the City University of New York and has been involved in several other Chelsea House projects, including the series REVOLUTIONARY WAR LEADERS, COLONIAL LEADERS, and YOUR GOVERNMENT.